B U Z Z

HOLY LAND
A SUBURBAN MEMOIR

D. J. Waldie

St. Martin's Griffin
New York

www.stmartins.com

Library of Congress Cataloging-in-Publication Data

Waldie, D. J.
Holy land : a suburban memoir / D. J. Waldie.
p. cm.
Originally published: New York : W. W. Norton, 1996.
ISBN 0-312-16864-0
EAN 978-0312-16864-3
1. Waldie, D. J. 2. Lakewood (Calif.)—Social life and
customs. 3. Lakewood (Calif.)—Biography.
4. Suburban life—California—Lakewood. I. Title.

[F869.L217W35 1997]
979.4'94—dc21 97-16854
CIP

First published in the United States
by W. W. Norton & Company Inc.

10 9 8

ACKNOWLEDGMENTS

My neighbors, former neighbors, and members of my family are named in this book. Some of them are, or were, public figures. They have foregone the choice of anonymity.

Some of those named in this book are dead, and cannot be slandered by my failure to tell their stories accurately.

Some others suffered intensely to make themselves vulnerable to the judgments in this book. I cannot think of the strengths and weaknesses of their lives without shame and wonder.

Some names of my friends and neighbors are given in full, by those who have allowed me that privilege. Some names are only an anonymous letter.

Behind the anonymity is a whole life, however, not merely an example. I have tried to tell the small part of their stories I know, and to respect as much of their privacy as I can.

Lois Craig, senior lecturer in the Department of Urban Studies and Planning at the Massachusetts Institute of Technology, looked at the aerial photographs of Lakewood and saw how they had framed all future views of my city and of suburbs generally.

Her analysis of the iconography of suburban places, in *Design Quarterly 186*, provided a point of departure for this book. I am greatly in her debt for the generosity and breadth of her ideas.

Portions of this book previously appeared in the *Kenyon Review*, the *Georgetown Review*, and the *Massachusetts Review*.

Steven Carter, Marilyn Hacker, Paul Jenkins, and David Lynn were sympathetic editors who were willing to include early drafts of some sections of this book in their publications.

I am particularly indebted to Marilyn Hacker and David Lynn of the *Kenyon Review*, who understood that this work is not a well-made story, and to Paul Jenkins of the *Massachusetts Review*, who sensitively combined the words and pictures of *Holy Land* for the first time.

A selection of forty-two essays and four photographs from *Holy Land* was published in 1995 as a special section of BUZZ magazine.

The entire staff of BUZZ—particularly editors Allan Mayer, Greg Critser, and Renée Vogel—were extraordinarily accommodating in presenting this part of *Holy Land.*

Grateful acknowledgment is made here for permission from each of these magazines to reprint the previously published portions of *Holy Land,* substantially modified and rearranged for this book.

I received a National Endowment for the Arts fellowship in Creative Nonfiction in 1994, which greatly helped in the completion of the manuscript of *Holy Land.*

Special thanks are due Alexander Ooms of the National Endowment for the Arts for his kind assistance, as well as Bret Lott and Lucha Corpi of the 1994 NEA Fiction/Nonfiction panel.

Encouragement also came from Ray Potter of Princeton University Press and Randy Burger of Cal Poly Pomona. They took an early interest in these suburban stories that paralleled in some measure their boyhoods in Southern California.

Among those who gave the gift of their time to read early versions of these stories are Emily Adams, Howard Chambers, Killarney Clarey, Brad Crenshaw, Thomas McGonigle, Deborah Gorlin, Liam and Mary Alice McLoughlin, Sandi Ruyle, Jane Sommerville, Sheryl Musicant Stewart, Michael and Patricia Stover, and Peggy Young. Janine Perkins was my invaluable research assistant.

Kevin Starr, the California State Librarian and a historian of Southern California, also offered his encouragement in the latter stages of writing this book.

The members of the Lakewood Rotary Club and the management association of Lakewood city employees kindly gave me time at their meetings to discuss some of the themes in this book and to read some of its sections.

Librarians at the County of Los Angeles Angelo M. Iacoboni Library in Lakewood, particularly Donna Walters and Linda Gahan, provided invaluable help in locating original materials. The Long Beach Library's local history collection, through the assistance of Librarian Claudine Burnett, supplied much of the information about early Long Beach.

Bill Hillburg, a columnist for the *Long Beach Press-Telegram* who has been chronicling the submerged history of southeast Los Angeles County for many years, was a wealth of information about the origins of the community in which I live.

Equally important was access to the records of the City of Lakewood. This was generously provided by my colleagues at Lakewood City Hall.

Julie Aharoni and Karen Kennedy, granddaughters of Louis Boyar, did me the great kindness of recognizing their beloved grandfather in those sections of *Holy Land* that deal with the original developers of Lakewood.

Jack Metzgar, who is writing a history of unionization and his family's role in the steelworkers' union, kindly read and commented on several sections of this book while they were still in manuscript.

Bringing this book to the attention of editors was due to the persistence of Chris Calhoun of Sterling Lord Literistic. His conviction that these stories matter eased the work of writing them.

Bringing this book to press was due to Jill Bialosky, my editor at Norton. It took her skill to make this a publishable book.

Joan Didion quoted from the first of these essays in an article about Lakewood in *The New Yorker* in July 1993. I am indebted to her support of this book and for the gift of her time, when I burdened her with early drafts of some sections of *Holy Land*.

Gary Young of *Greenhouse Review Press* made this book possible.

He first suggested the idea of maps and grids in a poem about my life in Lakewood. He was an attentive reader and editor during the book's development between 1990 and 1995. Nearly all that is good here shows his passion and wisdom.

To him, once more, much is owed.

I wrote this book for Maureen Rose McLoughlin and Catherine Grace McLoughlin, to whom I have already begun to tell these stories.

February 1996   *D. J. Waldie*
Lakewood, California

HOLY LAND

1

That evening he thought he was becoming his habits, or—
even more—he thought he was becoming the grid he knew.

He knew his suburb's first 17,500 houses had been built
in less than three years. He knew what this must have cost,
but he did not care.

The houses still worked.

He thought of them as middle class even though 1,100-
square-foot tract houses on streets meeting at right angles
are not middle class at all.

Middle-class houses are the homes of people who would
not live here.

2

In a suburb that is not exactly middle class, the necessary illusion is predictability.

3

When he thinks of his parents, he remembers them as they were in their early middle age—energetic, strong, and more capable than any other adult he knew.

He is older now than his parents had been then, and he is less competent than his father and mother seemed to him, even less competent than they were in fact.

This thought rarely troubles him.

4

Whether liked or disliked, it is for himself, and not for what he has done, that others judge him. He has generally done nothing at all.

5

It rained once for an entire week in 1953, when I was five. The flat streets flooded. Schools closed. Only the rain happened, while I waited at the window.

Waiting was one of the first things I understood fully. Rain and the hydrogen bomb were two aspects of the same loss.

6

Moral choice does not enter his thinking.

He believes, however, that each of us is crucified. His own crucifixion is the humiliation of living the life he has made for himself.

7

You and I grew up in these neighborhoods when they were an interleaving of houses and fields that were soon to be filled with more houses.

A particular sound marked the boundary of the neighborhood. It was the barking of dogs near full dark in summer. Do you remember it?

The flat barking skipped from block to block, unhinged from causes, not necessarily your neighbors' dog, but their dog too.

That sound became the whole neighborhood clearing its throat before going to bed and sleep.

8

At some point in your story grief presents itself.

Now, for the first time, your room is empty, not merely unoccupied.

9

Before they put a grid over it, and restrained the ground from indifference, any place was as good as any other.

10

There were only a few trees here, eighty years ago. They were eucalyptus trees near some farm buildings, deliberately planted for shade. Men waited under them before their work began.

The men's faces were brown on the jaw and chin, and pale above.

In the fields, only the upper part of a man's face is shaded by his hat, salt-stained along the base of the crown.

Work began for the men when each man pulled himself to a high wooden seat above a harvester's moving rack of teeth.

This contraption was pulled by twenty mules, straining as the men joked.

11

The grid is the plan above the earth. It is a compass of possibilities.

12

In 1949, three developers bought 3,500 acres of Southern California farmland.

They planned to build something that was not exactly a city.

In 1950, before the work of roughing the foundations and pouring concrete began, the three men hired a young photographer with a single-engine plane to document their achievement from the air.

The photographer flew when the foundations of the first houses were poured. He flew again when the framing was done and later, when the roofers were nearly finished. He flew over the shell of the shopping center that explains this and many other California suburbs.

The three developers were pleased with the results. The black-and-white photographs show immense abstractions on ground the color of the full moon.

Some of the photographs appeared in *Fortune* and other magazines. The developers bound enlargements in a handsome presentation book. I have several pages from one of the copies.

The photographs celebrate house frames precise as cells in a hive and stucco walls fragile as an unearthed bone.

Seen from above, the grid is beautiful and terrible.

13

Four of the young man's photographs became the definition of this suburb, and then of suburbs generally.

The photographs look down before the moving vans arrived, and before you and I learned to play hide-and-seek beneath the poisonous oleander trees.

Architectural critics and urban theorists reprinted the photographs in books with names like *God's Own Junk-yard*. Forty years later, the same four photographs still stand for the places in which most of us live.

The photographs were images of the developers' crude pride. They report that the grid, briefly empty of associations, is just a pattern predicting itself.

The theorists and critics did not look again, forty years later, to see the intersections or calculate in them the joining of interests, limited but attainable, like the leasing of chain stores in a shopping mall.

14

In the Los Angeles basin, the possibility of rain is ignored until the rain falls. Since it hardly ever rains, ignorance has prevailed as climate.

15

The local newspaper in 1956 used a picture to show how much had changed. This picture "Harvesting, 1900."

It shows a team of mules, a combine harvester, the field,

and the men. The mules are sawteeth of black; the combine is a grand contraption in gray; the field is all design.

You cannot make out the men. They are patterns in the photograph.

16

My father's kindness was as pure and indifferent as a certain kind of saint's.

My father did not have a passion for his giving; it came from him, perhaps after much spiritual calculation, as a product might come from a conveyor belt.

The houses in this suburb were built the same way. As many as a hundred a day were begun between 1950 and 1952, more than five hundred a week. No two floor plans were built next to each other; no neighbor had to stare into his reflection across the street.

Teams of men built the houses.

Some men poured concrete into the ranks of foundations from mixing trucks waiting in a mile-long line. Other men threw down floors nailed with pneumatic hammers, tilted up the framing, and scaled the rafters with cedar shingles lifted by conveyer belts from the beds of specially built trucks.

You are mistaken if you consider this a criticism, either of my father or the houses.

17

Construction crews in thirty-man teams built the rows of houses. Each team of workmen was subdivided by specialty.

One man with a pneumatic hammer nailed subfloors on five houses a day. The framers finished lengths of precut lumber with new, electric saws. Another crew operated a power door hanger.

Rough plaster laid by one crew was smoothed a few minutes later by another.

Subcontractors delivered construction materials in exact amounts directly to each building site. Expediters coordinated the work from radio-equipped cars.

The foreman used a loudspeaker to direct the movement of his men.

18

Mr. F laid rafters for hundreds of these houses. According to Mr. F, it didn't take much skill.

The most experienced men did the framing, by assembling pieces that had been precut at the mill. Laying rafters only required knowing how to swing a hammer all day.

By 1951, the construction bosses had hired more than four thousand workmen. They were mostly unskilled veterans still in their twenties. They learned how to lay rafters— or they didn't learn—in a day or two.

The men who put up with the pace and the monotony stayed on. They earned about a dollar an hour.

19

According to Mr. F, the speed of the work depended on a gimmick called a "scaffold jack." The jack made it possible for two men to begin laying rafters with no time wasted in setting up a freestanding scaffold.

Instead, braces cut from channel iron, each fitted with two bars of sawteeth that bit into the wood stud, could be nailed up quickly on the skeletal frame of the house.

Each jack held a short length of two-by-four. On these projecting arms the roofers laid the planks on which they stood to work.

The jacks transmitted the weight of the cantilevered scaffold planks to the studs of the house frame. The planks and the men themselves made the jack bite securely into the wood.

Simple forces supported the planks, the men, and the scaffold jacks hanging about six feet above the ground.

20

The scaffold jacks were ingenious and economical. A pair could be cut and welded together from a single, eighteen-inch length of channel iron.

The process of setting the jacks up on the studs and laying the scaffold planks took the men only a few minutes.

The jack let each completed house supply the support for the next construction step. It was like lifting yourself by your bootstraps, Mr. F said.

The scaffold jack didn't last.

In the 1960s, the standard two-by-four stud was pared down to reduce lumber costs. Today, a two-by-four is one-and-a-half inches by three-and-a-half inches.

Mr. F says a scaffold jack would snap one of these new studs in two.

21

If the workmen looked up from laying rafters, they saw a row of houses with bundles of shingles being lifted by conveyor belts to shinglers on the roof. Beyond them was a row of house frames being sheathed in tar paper and chicken wire. Beyond them was another row of houses gray with new stucco. Beyond that row would be another row of houses, only a few days older, being painted.

Behind them, nearly out of sight, would be a street of finished houses, forty-six to a block.

To the workmen, suspended on the scaffold, these finished houses must have seemed out of place and very still.

22

The *Los Angeles Daily News* described the construction of the houses as a huge assembly line.

23

Mr. F made the city a detailed scale model of a garage being framed.

He wanted to show school children, who sometimes tour city hall, how efficiently he had laid rafters as a young man.

His model includes a set of full-size scaffold jacks mounted on two uprights with a short length of scaffold plank between them.

The model garage is mounted on a table Mr. F built. The entire display, including the table and model, is about five-and-a-half feet high.

The roof of the scale model is about half laid, so that the pattern of rafters can be seen.

Mr. F put a Ken doll on the model scaffold to show how the roofers worked. Ken is holding a tiny hammer.

24

Daily life here has an inertia that people believe in.

In the city's most recent opinion survey, 92 percent of the residents believe this suburb is a desirable place in which to live.

Such is the attraction of suburbs. You look out your

kitchen window to the bedroom window of your neighbor precisely fifteen feet away.

25

The distance between my house and yours is a separation the suburb's designers carefully planned. It is one of the principal factors in determining the number of houses per acre in a subdivision.

The number of houses per acre is the subdivision's yield. This is a measure of its profitability, which is not the number of houses that can be sold, but the subdivision's population density.

Density is what developers sell to the builders of shopping centers.

26

The average number of houses per acre in prewar subdivisions had been about five.

In the suburb where I live, begun in 1950, the number of houses per acre is eight.

The houses were designed by an architect named Paul Duncan.

27

You leave the space between the houses uncrossed. You rarely go across the street, which is forty feet wide.

You are grateful for the distance. It is as if each house on

your block stood on its own enchanted island, fifty feet wide
by one hundred feet long.

People come and go from it, your parents mostly and your
friends. Your parents arrive like pilgrims.

But the island is remote. You occasionally hear the
sounds of anger. You almost never hear the sounds of love.

You hear, always at night, the shifting of the uprights, the
sagging of ceiling joists, and the unpredictable ticking of
the gas heater.

28

What is beautiful here?

The calling of a mourning dove, and others answering
from yard to yard. Perhaps this is the only thing beautiful
here.

29

What more can you expect of me than the stories I am now
telling?

30

In 1954, in the local newspaper:

"The nearby areas are among the best protected in the
United States against the damaging effects of atom and
hydrogen bombs. This was brought out in reports yesterday
from the Mutual Aid District, which has a protective arm
around the newest city in America. There is a trained army

of damage control people ready to leap to duty. Our speaker said, "We used to have about an hour to get ready from the time of the first alert until the time bombs would fall, then the time was 15 minutes or less. Now we know that with jets flying at excessive speed, and guided missiles, we may have no time at all. We must be on our toes at all times, as though the enemy would strike with the next breath."

31

The city has a war memorial given to it by the Marine Corps in 1956, a souvenir of Korea. It is a Douglas F-3D fighter painted above and below in the gray and white of a shark.

In the mid-1950s, the Marine Corps donated gutted fighters to cities if they would haul one away to a public place and have the plane repainted at intervals.

Douglas Aircraft, the region's biggest employer, called the F-3D the *Skyknight*.

There is the head of an Indian painted on the side of our *Skyknight*. The Indian may be a Navajo. He looks like the Indian on a Navajo Freight Lines truck. Both Indians have blue eyes.

The Marines gave the city the jet fighter, lacking any operating gear, as a pure husk, as a toy.

And it was, for a time.

The city had the shell of the jet brought here from the next county and laid it belly down, with no landing gear, flat on the scraped ground in a new park. Children played on it.

For two years the F-3D lay as if its pilot had made an oddly successful, wheels-up landing between the jungle gym and the swing set.

32

Almost at once, the F-3D began to hurt children, who broke arms and legs jumping from its wings.

To protect the children, the city put its jet on a twelve-foot high, white, concrete pylon that swept the F-3D forward, like a mid-1950s hood ornament. Up there is where the future lay safely.

The county construction crew fixed the plane in a gentle climb. It does not look ridiculous or particularly military. Besides, sycamore trees obscure it from the boulevard.

The pylon was marked with one plaque—a dedication to the Korean War dead of the city. The plaque has the names of city council members on it and no one else's.

33

Every Memorial Day, we go out to the park and honor our dead.

We gather under the wings of the war memorial with some members of the American Legion, the Veterans of Foreign Wars, and the Disabled American Veterans. The women's auxiliaries participate. The mix of men and women is about equal.

In recent years the number of those attending has grown. About 150 veterans and the wives and widows of veterans attend.

A unit from the high school Navy ROTC presents the colors. The Legion post commander says a few words. The mayor says a few words. A guest speaker chosen by the Legion makes a patriotic speech.

They read the names of all the old men of the Legion, VFW, and DAV who have died in the past year. It is a fairly long list.

The city council members read the names of young men from this suburb who died in Vietnam. It is always the same list of thirty-two names.

34

Beneath Mrs. A's house, the military, defense contractors, and the makers of nuclear waste toil and murder. She feels the thudding of their engines.

She knows that the dead from the nearby aircraft plant are secretly buried there.

The hidden trainloads of atomic waste kill her lawn and

bubble to the surface in pools of red liquid to stain her garage floor.

A city council member once went out to look, and Mrs. A fell weeping into his startled arms.

35

The Army Corps of Engineers, in league with the Douglas Aircraft Company, tunnels beneath Mrs. A's house so that it threatens to slide into the pit.

Mrs. A wrote President Carter. He held back the Corps of Engineers during his term. President Reagan had no such power; the toppling of her house into the Army's excavation resumed.

In Mrs. A's closet was a string. When she pulled it, the digging stopped. But only for a while.

I am aware of this because, as a city official, I receive Mrs. A's extensive correspondence.

36

Mrs. A writes that the NASA moon shots were financed by the distribution of a pornographic film of her rape by a McDonald's fry cook and a professional football team.

Mrs. A wants the showings stopped.

37

I once received a well-printed flyer, with photographs and charts, calling on men of good will in both the United States and the Soviet Union to undertake a manned mission to Mars and, once there, to conduct a grand worship service for Jesus Christ.

The author of the flyer, a retired military officer, called this ceremony on Mars "un beau geste."

38

On another occasion, I received two sheets of ledger paper big enough for keeping hundreds of financial entries.

The sheets were filled on both sides and from edge to edge with minute, clear handwriting. There were thousands of words in one, enormous paragraph.

There is a neurological disorder, a kind of epilepsy, which compels its sufferers to write.

39

Someone from the state mental hospital sends the city a theme song.

Someone else writes of divine retribution from Canada and the loss of the love of her husband.

Another resident covers her doors and windows against the rays, and paints her house blue in welcome for alien visitors.

Red traffic signals persecute a man on his way to work at night. He wants the city to make them all green.

Another man carves the Venus de Milo from the stump of a tree rooted in his front yard. He receives considerable attention from the newspapers.

Mrs. A argues that the cable television company wrecked the roof of her garden shed as the company's men strung their cable to the electric pole behind her house.

The men use a handful of lug nuts threaded on a cord to throw the free end of the coaxial cable from yard to yard. Perhaps they did hit Mrs. A's roof.

She comes before the members of the city's cable television commission and demands restitution. The commissioners agree, and the company pays.

40

Mr. H has covered his yard, a few blocks over from mine, with junk. There may be as many as ten tons or as few as six. The city cannot tell. The mix of dead machinery and used building supplies changes over time.

City inspectors routinely go over to look.

Mr. H's front and back yards teem with equipment that no longer works, with his own castoffs and with other people's.

Mr. H protests that he needs all of it. He has construction plans. He is working on a room addition. He is an advocate of recycling.

He also claims that people bring him their junk against his will. Can he help it if they leave their broken washers and used lumber on his lawn?

Mr. H operates construction equipment during the day. He drives a pickup truck late at night.

The tons of junk gather without effort. The lonely debris of the city finds a home at Mr. H's house.

He starts to call himself a landscape consultant.

41

After a while, Mr. H's neighbors complain. They have hesitated years before they call city hall. The neighbors say they don't want to "make trouble."

They see a ripple on the surface of their neighborhood, a defection from predictability.

On their behalf, the city's building department spends the next ten years looking into Mr. H's yard.

Assistant planners, code enforcement officers, and department directors visit. They take photographs and arrange meetings with Mr. H and, later, with his wife and other members of his family.

Mr. H is counseled. He is offered help. He is given options. He is warned that he has broken several laws.

In the municipal code book in the city clerk's office are fifteen pages of ordinances about property maintenance, nuisance abatement, clearing sidewalks, and covering garbage cans.

The city with its codes cannot make Mr. H a good citizen.

42

In the suburbs, a manageable life depends on a compact among neighbors. The unspoken agreement is an honest hypocrisy.

Pages of ordinances in the municipal code are never enforced. They are, in fact, unenforceable. You do not need a law to keep your neighbor from walling his yard with used refrigerators.

When he does, what law would have restrained him?

43

This suburb was thrown up on plowed-under bean fields beginning in early 1950. No theorist or urban planner had the experience then to gauge how thirty thousand former GIs and their wives would take to frame and stucco houses on small, rectangular lots next to hog farms and dairies.

In Long Beach, some businessmen assumed the result would be a slum. Others wondered if it would be a ghost town.

Someone asked the eager promoter sent by the developers, "Who will you sell all those houses to—the jack rabbits?"

Had you seen the delicate houses then, going up on the tract's light gray soil, the ground scraped clean and as flat as Kansas, you might have wondered, too.

44

This is not a garden suburb. The streets do not curve or offer vistas.

The street grid always intersects at right angles. The north-south roads are avenues. The east-west roads are streets. The four-lane highways in either compass orientation are boulevards.

The city planted some of these with eucalyptus trees and red crape myrtle on narrow, well-tended medians and parkway strips.

People passing through the city often mention the trees. They never mention the pattern over which they pass.

45

The streets in my city are a fraction of a larger grid, anchored to one in Los Angeles. That grid was laid out in September 1781.

The Los Angeles grid is a copy of one carried from Mexico City to an anonymous stretch of river bank by Colonel Felipe de Neve, governor of California.

The grid the Spanish colonel carried to the nonexistent Los Angeles in 1781 originally came from a book in the Archive of the Indies in Seville. The book prescribed the exact orientation of the streets, the houses, and the public places for all the colonial settlements in the Spanish Americas.

That grid came from God.

46

"Stop counting, mother," I said, bending over her hospital bed.

And she stopped on three. All afternoon she had been telling numbers as she died.

She kept saying, "3, 2, 5, 3, 2."

I said, "Stop counting, mother." She stopped again on three.

What were they? Were they a telephone number or a street address?

They were coordinates for a map I did not have.

47

Three-quarters of the United States is platted on a grid that follows the lines of longitude and latitude across the continent.

The Land Ordinance of 1785, written by Thomas Jefferson, provided for the survey and sale of mile-square sections of land in the wilderness west of the Ohio River. The survey specified the strict orientation of these sections to the cardinal points of the compass.

Jefferson's grid, extending endlessly, explains why so many western states have sharp edges.

48

After more than ten years, Mr. H has exhausted all of the city's administrative procedures. These are the conferences, warnings, and deadline extensions that are the city's sidesteps to a confrontation.

Mr. H's case is turned over to the district attorney's office. He is brought before a judge and ordered to clean up his property.

Mr. H tries to comply with the judge's order. The junk dwindles from his front yard over the next three months, and then again at night it gathers.

I think of his wife's embarrassment and his grown children's anger. I think of his neighbors.

Mr. H has another hearing and is found in contempt of court. Mr. H goes to jail.

In all, Mr. H spends more than sixty days in the county jail in downtown Los Angeles. He spends more time in jail than a check forger, a first-time car thief, or a man convicted of assault.

While he is in jail, Mr. H's family clears his front and back yards of the inevitable lumber and broken equipment.

When he returns from jail, the yard is empty, and the bank forecloses Mr. H's mortgage.

His house is taken from him.

49

My father died behind a well-made, wooden bathroom door.

It is a three-panel door. Each panel is nearly square, twenty-one inches wide by nineteen inches high. From edge to edge, the door is twenty-eight inches wide.

All the original doors in the house are the same—grids of three rectangles surrounded by a raised framework.

Painted white, as they are now, each square of each door is molded in the light by a right angle of shadow.

The doors in my house are abstract and ordinary. The bathroom door is now forty-seven years old. My father was sixty-nine.

50

The house where I still live, and where my father died, predates the building of the rest of this city. The houses in my neighborhood were built at the start of the Second World War for workers at the Douglas Aircraft plant in Long Beach, about two miles away.

That was far enough for the houses to survive a Japanese air raid on the Douglas plant.

The War Department covered Douglas Aircraft in acres of camouflage developed by the movie studios to mimic tract houses. The false suburb, made of wire and plaster, successfully blended with the real suburb farther up the boulevard.

No one who lived there questioned that the War Department could make these real houses the target of deceived Japanese bombers.

51

The houses in my neighborhood were built of lumber that was seasoned before the war. Today, carpenters and plumbers have to work hard at drilling through the studs.

The frames of the houses are overbuilt. Adding a second story is easy.

The bathroom door in my house is shut with a cheap replacement lock, the kind that dads pick up at the hardware store. It is a lock with a small hole in the outside knob so the door can be opened with a narrow-blade screw driver if a four-year-old locks himself in.

I didn't have a narrow-blade screw driver.

The seasoned wood of almost fifty years is Douglas fir. The door did not break when I hit it with my shoulder. The cheap catch did not spring from the lock plate in the door jamb.

And my father's legs braced the door shut as he sat on the floor, his back against the bathtub.

52

My house is not very far from the hospital where my mother died. It is about a mile.

Three years after her death, I rode to the hospital in the ambulance with my father's body. The ambulance turned left from my street, then left again on the boulevard, and then right to the hospital.

The boulevard bisects this suburb. The median is planted with a double row of sycamore trees paid for by the city's redevelopment agency. Because trees are thought to encourage business growth, the state's redevelopment law encourages cities to plant trees with borrowed money.

Both the boulevard and the city are named after a speculative subdivision laid out a dozen years before my parents' house was built.

College teachers, naval officers, and doctors built houses in this subdivision in the 1930s and 1940s. Its developer pointed out that the subdivision had "restrictions of an all-inclusive nature."

When the residents of the young suburb voted for incorporation as a city in 1954, these older neighborhoods retreated into the city of Long Beach.

The residents were afraid they would be caretakers of the slum my city was supposed to become.

53

William A. Clark of Montana bought 8,139 acres of farmland from the Bixby family in 1897. They sold him a small corner of a remnant of the land given to Manuel Nieto in 1784 for his service as a soldier of Spain in California.

The governor of California gave Nieto all the land between the San Gabriel and the Santa Ana rivers and from the Pacific Ocean to the foothills of the San Gabriel Mountains.

The grant had a pointless grandeur. It was four or five hundred square miles.

The land belonged to Manuel Nieto in the form of a drawing called a *diseño*. It was a sketch that showed three vague rivers, the mountains, and the Pacific Ocean.

Nieto built an adobe house of one or two rooms by a spring, at the foot of some low hills, a few miles north of my house.

Nieto never visited the twenty-five miles of white sand beach he owned. He never made a map of his property or knew precisely where he lived on it.

54

In Montana, William A. Clark owned silver mines. In Arizona, he owned one of the nation's richest copper mines.

In California, he owned an anonymous stretch of alluvial plain that was neither beach front nor an oil field.

Clark formed the Montana Land Company with his brother to grow sugar beets because a protective tariff encouraged domestic production. Wire worm infestation eventually ruined the crop.

The government also lowered the tariff, and foreign suppliers drove the price of sugar down.

Beginning in 1928, the Montana Land Company began leasing its land to tenant farmers who grew acres of lima beans, alfalfa, and carrots.

55

He sat on the edge of his bed in the middle room and waited for his father to die. His father walked down the hall to take a shower. It was after 11 p.m.

He was rehearsing his father's death in his imagination.

The death of his father, even more than the death of his mother three years before, could free him from an obligation.

His father's goodness was part of that obligation. His father's refusals were a part of it, too.

His father died on Sunday night, the 15th of August and the feast of the Assumption of the Blessed Virgin Mary.

56

I waited on the edge of my bed in the middle bedroom, in a room that had been mine only since I started college.

Rooms are small in houses that have less than eleven

hundred square feet of living area. The room I slept in was ten feet by ten feet.

All the bedrooms in my house open on a hallway barely thirteen feet long. My father's bedroom and the back bedroom are both ten feet by thirteen feet.

I heard my father pass down the hall by the closed door of my room as I waited. It was late Sunday night.

My father passed by on his way to the bathroom to take a shower. He showered at night. I showered in the morning. We had not agreed on this arrangement.

I waited for my father to take his shower so I could use the bathroom and get ready for bed. While I waited, I thought of his death.

Later, I heard a groan. It was not remarkable. I heard the shower door slam. I waited for the sound of water running.

Some time later, I looked for a narrow-blade screwdriver. I tried to force the bathroom door with my shoulder.

Later still, I saw his corpse.

57

In my city, a fire engine arrives before the paramedic unit.

The fire fighters and the city's three fire stations are part of a regional fire protection district covering nearly the entire county. All fire fighters are trained as Emergency Medical Technicians, a level of medical training just below that of a paramedic.

The fire department's plan to train fire fighters to respond to medical emergencies was tested in this suburb, as were other innovations in public safety.

Also, there are hardly any fires.

58

In forty-one years, fewer than a dozen houses have burned to the ground here. Fire damage rarely totals more than three or four hundred thousand dollars a year.

The successful fires are sometimes deliberate.

A woman nine blocks west of my street woke up early one morning and went to the garage. She took a gallon of gasoline, fuel for her husband's lawn mower, and poured the gasoline around the foundation of the house.

She set the gasoline on fire and waited quietly in the dawn for the flames to build.

A newspaper carrier on his bike saw the fire next, about a half-hour later. By then, the eaves of the roof had caught.

When the fire engines arrived, the trees in the front yard had turned black, and the woman had already been taken away.

59

The ambulance—a contract service of the County of Los Angeles—arrived at my father's death about half an hour after the county fire engine.

By then, the fire fighters had delivered my father from the bathroom and had laid him out on the living room carpet. I continued to sit on the edge of my bed in the middle room as they tried to restore the rhythm of my father's heart.

The fire fighters were dressed in the stiff canvas jackets that protect them from the flames they rarely have to put out.

The men bent over my father awkwardly, adjusting the electrocardiograph and receiving radioed instructions from the hospital emergency room.

My father's heart was unruly. The beats only flickered through the monitor. The defibrillator the fire fighters used only gave his heart another spasm, a shudder he did not feel.

When the fire fighters were done, I rode with the body in the ambulance, its siren shouting.

My brother brought me back from the hospital. I spent that night in the empty house, as I continue to spend each night at home.

60

He could not choose to deny his father, even less his father's beliefs. These have become as material to him as the stucco-over-chicken-wire from which these houses are made.

It is not a question of denying the city in which he lives, though he doubts his father cared much for living in it. He doubts if his father cared for much of anything you would find familiar at all.

"I am still here," he often tells himself. This is how he has resurrected his father's obligations, which he sometimes mistakes for his father's faith.

"I will never go away," he once told the girl he loved, because it suited her desperation and his notion of the absurd.

Loving Christ badly was finally the best he could do.

61

There are ugly deaths. And then, there are the dead.

You and I, who grew up in the years after the Second World War, saw enough reasons for dying. We saw the movie versions of storm troopers, kamikaze pilots, quislings, and the cowards who would not face them.

Our parents' war lapped over us in gray shadows from television sets in darkened living rooms. That lunar blue-gray was the emotional color of violence and the dead it produced.

When images of real war appeared, in programs like *Victory at Sea*, the ashen dead were never less than themselves.

When I was called to the hospital table on which my father was laid, after his dying had moved throughout his body, he was the color of television's black-and-white dead.

62

My father died of tachycardia. My mother had died of congestive heart failure.

It seems that my father's heart finally raced ahead of him, while my mother's had lagged behind.

63

After forty years of development, there are 26,766 places to live in this suburb. On any day, about 2 percent are vacant. No house stands empty for long.

An empty house is a source of worry. A sheriff's unit will

drive by at noon. Neighbors call city hall with complaints about weeds in the lawn and the unchecked garden.

Most empty houses are owned by out-of-town landlords with skipped renters. Occasionally, an empty house will hide a hunched and blackening corpse, in bed, on the kitchen floor, or in the hall.

A letter carrier puts mail through a slot in the door to which no one else comes. The house, in this climate, only grows dusty.

Eventually someone wonders, when the weeds have gone too long.

Some neighbor's husband, with only a little persuasion, will try doors and attempt to look in. A braver one, standing on a ladder, will break the window over the kitchen sink.

In a week or two, with the lawn mowed, the house will be up for sale.

64

Every block is divided into the common grid of fifty-by-one-hundred-foot lots.

All the houses are about 1,100 square feet.

The houses are on ground so flat that the average grade across the city's nine-and-a-half square miles is less than a foot. Tree roots, bulging into a gutter, pond dark water down half a block.

65

These houses went up cheaply on fields cut to stubble only hours before construction began.

Veterans needed no down payment, and the Federal

Housing Authority guaranteed loans at four percent interest for up to thirty years.

Nonveterans paid $695 down.

Mortgage payments began at $46.98 a month for a two-bedroom house and $53.50 for one with three.

The two-bedroom houses sold for $7,575. The three-bedroom houses sold for $8,525.

The first unit of the new subdivision was ready for sale in March 1950. Rows of concrete foundations surrounded the one remaining bean field where the ground had been broken for the shopping center.

The developers were anxious to identify their development, so remote from any city. They put a steel oil derrick at the edge of the last field, mounted a war-surplus beacon at the top, and strung the derrick's legs with more electric lights.

At night, a hundred feet above the implausibly level ground, the light could be seen for miles.

66

Buyers did not require encouragement. When the sales office opened on a cloudless Palm Sunday in April 1950, twenty-five thousand people were waiting.

Almost as many showed up on Easter Sunday, and on the weekends through May and June.

Couples waited in line to be led in and out of a row of seven model houses, the first time that a street of model houses was used to sell a subdivision.

Young men from the nearby junior college, recruited from the athletic department, acted as guides to the unfamiliar experience.

The models were furnished by the Aaron Schultz furniture store in Long Beach. Each model was decorated in one of four styles—Maple, Traditional, Modern, and Provincial.

At night, the model houses were lighted by rows of flood lamps.

The seven model yards were planted with mature shrubs and full lawns. The landscaping made the houses look about three years old.

Buyers waited in a second line, some watching their children in a supervised playground. When it was their turn, they went inside the barn-like sales office with its displays of floor plans and rows of cubicles, each with a desk faced by two chairs.

67

The city in which I live is the second oldest "new" suburb in the nation.

The Levittown on Long Island was built on former potato fields beginning in 1946, but it was planned as a smaller development and it did not surround a shopping center.

In 1950, Don Rochlen, the publicist for the developers, insisted on these two points when he spoke to reporters from Long Beach and Los Angeles.

68

The three developers learned from the experience of Levittown that the new home owners were unprepared to set up housekeeping.

The developers offered to include an O'Keefe & Merritt

gas range, a Norge refrigerator, and a Bendix "Economat" washing machine in the price of each house they sold.

The additional monthly charge, added to the mortgage, was nine dollars for each appliance.

69

The sales force was thirty-five young men. On weekends, when most of the houses were sold, the salesmen worked day and evening shifts from 9 a.m. to 10 p.m.

The salesmen did not encourage buyers to linger. Husbands and wives selected a floor plan, signed a sales contract, looked at a map of the tract, and accepted the house they were assigned.

The salesman got a thirty-five-dollar commission on each sale.

In the office, among displays showing construction photographs and sales brochures, the houses may have retreated slightly.

If the buyers hesitated, astonished at what they were about to do, the salesman looked past them to the line of other husbands and wives watching their children in the bright light.

70

Some buyers came back to the construction site on the next weekend to see their house.

They picked their way through the confusion of sandy streets, past quiet road graders and stacks of precut lumber, looking for their house by the pattern of its floor plan.

There were fourteen of these at the beginning, with twenty-one exterior designs and thirty-nine combinations of stucco and wood trim.

Buyers tried to match the skeleton of Douglas fir to the watercolor rendering of the model in the sales brochure, with its printer's process blue sky and spindly eucalyptus tree.

As explained in the brochure, their house came with a Waste King electric garbage disposer, oak floors, service porch, stainless-steel kitchen counter, and a stainless-steel double sink.

Each house would have a tree, chosen by the developers, planted in the parkway in front of it.

This was "the city as new as tomorrow."

71

My mother would have preferred a Japanese house of paper and satinwood—a house without anything that could be taken from her.

She had hoped for a life like that.

My father's mother, on the other hand, had hoped that her seven sons would all become priests.

72

The average age of the wives in the new suburb was twenty-six. The average age of the husbands was thirty-two.

Most families made between $4,000 and $7,000 a year. The average income was $5,100. That was $2,000 higher than the national average in 1950.

My father made $4,600 that year, working as a laboratory assistant for the Gas Company.

Seventy-five percent of the buyers were purchasing their first house. They used credit to buy a car and furniture. By 1953, 98 percent of the households had a television set.

No one had any money.

73

In 1952, a reporter for the local paper interviewed an average resident of the new suburb. He lived on Hayter Street. He had a wife, a son, and a daughter.

He was thirty-two. He earned $4,400 a year. Including property taxes and insurance, he paid $70 a month for his three-bedroom house.

He paid $19 a month on his new television set and $48 a month for his new furniture.

His wife knew only her next-door neighbors until she joined a sewing club on her block. There she met five more of her neighbors.

He and his wife were registered Democrats, but they had voted that November for Eisenhower.

He said he and his wife were looking for a church, but they didn't know which one.

They wanted to get involved in the community, he said, but they wanted to get the grass growing in their front yard first.

74

A majority of registered voters in the new suburb voted for Eisenhower in 1952.

75

There wasn't much crime in these neighborhoods.

If you had asked residents what their new community needed, many would have said it needed to control dogs.

Dogs were bought, or picked up from the county animal shelter, because parents thought it would be good for their children.

Dogs would teach responsibility.

They didn't. Most children were too young to train a dog, and parents didn't have enough time.

Some dogs ran loose during the day. Some bit mail carriers and delivery men. Some were just a general nuisance, digging in gardens and fouling lawns.

Young dogs that were tied up barked or howled incessantly. The constant noise pitted neighbor against neighbor.

Because the new suburb was unincorporated, the county animal control department was responsible for picking up and impounding strays.

But the county could do nothing about barking dogs.

76

Parents wanted the county to do something about covering the open ditches between neighborhoods.

The ditches had been dug out by a backhoe when the houses were built, to drain the wetter parts of the new development.

When it rained, the ten-foot-deep ditches would fill with water.

In the spring, the ditches would fill with cattails and the tadpoles that boys would catch. They put the tadpoles in glass jars to watch them become frogs.

The ditches attracted boys in packs of four or five, as did any empty lot where there was enough room to dig.

One boy died when the fort he made of scrap lumber and dirt collapsed on him. Another boy drowned in a flooded sump.

77

Forty-five percent of the new suburb's population was less than nineteen years of age in 1953. Twenty-five percent was less than ten years old.

Some property owners worried about living among so many children. Parents wondered what would happen when their neighborhoods had thirty thousand teenagers.

They talked about the "juvenile crime problem," and wanted more parks built.

78

The houses in my neighborhood touch the ground lightly. There is no basement.

Foundations are hardly more than a foot deep. It took a bucket excavator only fifteen minutes to dig each one.

Carpenters followed and nailed up three-foot foundation forms as quickly as possible.

Workmen poured the concrete quickly, too. The crews poured 2,113 foundations in a hundred days. For every ten houses, they wasted enough concrete for the foundation of an eleventh.

The raised foundation of each house leaves an eighteen-inch crawl space beneath the floor.

My father went under there occasionally, to move an electrical outlet without the benefit of a city building permit.

The crawl space is partly lighted by vents in the foundation. From association, the pale wood of the joists beneath the floor has become the same gray color as the dirt.

79

The attic is different. At the ridge board, where the rafters join, there is just enough space for a grown man to stand slightly hunched.

My father rigged a light there, over the attic hatch in the hallway ceiling. Before you climb into the attic, you can turn the light on by reaching up and pulling a string tied to the socket chain.

In this light, the wood seems new. It still smells of sawn lumber.

My parents filled the attic with things we used every year, but only once a year—the aluminum Christmas tree, ornaments and lights, plastic houses for the train set, winter clothes, and vacation luggage.

The attic held things that were no longer used—my father's Navy uniforms, the love letters my mother sent him during the war, and the notebook he kept when he belonged to a Catholic religious order.

Despite the light, the attic is threatening to walk in, because only a few loose planks lie across the joists. A bad step will put your foot through a bedroom ceiling.

80

My house is largely a void.

The emptiness is not just in the span of the rooms or in the attic and foundation spaces. All the walls are hollow, too.

Houses in Southern California are built as sketchily as possible, while still able to shed rain. Walls are a thin, cement skin over absence.

Roofs are important here, but only when it rains. The rest is for modesty.

81

The outside walls are stucco, a mixture of sand and Portland cement.

The exterior coat is about an eighth-inch thick, with a ratio of four parts of sand to one part of cement.

The middle coat is three-eighths of an inch. The ratio of sand to cement is five to one.

The first layer of stucco—three-eighths of an inch of four parts of sand to one part cement—was quickly troweled over chicken wire. The wire was furred a quarter-inch from tarpaper sheets nailed to the outside edge of the studs.

The surface of a stucco house clings to this network of light wire and not to the wood frame. The wire intersections support the stucco over the empty span of the walls.

The brittle exterior of these houses is a little more than an inch thick.

82

The houses on my block have been painted so often that the grains of sand in the surface of the stucco have begun to disappear.

83

Behind the layers of stucco and tar paper are the vertical studs, pine two-by-fours sixteen inches apart. Spanning these are wooden members called fire blocks.

The fire blocks are not for support; they separate pockets of dead air inside the finished wall.

Fire blocks prevent the empty vertical space between each pair of studs from becoming a chimney that would carry a fire to the rafters and bring the house down.

Frame houses are based on a rough balance. The wood frame resists gravity's downward thrust of the heavy roof; the rafters nailed to the roof's ridge board brace the walls from falling outward.

84

Playing hide-and-seek once, just at sunset, I stood in the doorway of the darkened bedroom I shared with my older brother, knees actually knocking in fear.

85

My house was built by a real estate development company in 1942. The company built eleven hundred houses on land Clark Bonner had sold them.

The company built the houses for workers at the Douglas Aircraft plant.

My house was bought by a guard at the federal prison on Terminal Island in Long Beach.

When my parents bought the house from him in 1946, it was landscaped with a row of palm trees along the driveway. There was a rock garden behind the house.

The pile of rocks was higher than the wood fence around the yard. Whitewashed boulders from the San Gabriel River edged the front walk.

The guard had used men from the prison to plant the palm trees and build the rock garden.

It took my father months to remove the palms, which eventually would have towered over the house. He took down the rock garden and carried the boulders to the county dump in the trunk of his car.

The guard left behind several pieces of furniture, made by prisoners from scrap lumber.

My parents had to keep the furniture when they bought the house. They couldn't afford to replace it.

The furniture was in the room my brother and I shared. I still have some of the pieces.

86

This photograph is heavily retouched. A wood-body station wagon is posed in front of one of the model houses in the picture. Otherwise, the scene is deserted.

It is unclear if the photograph will help sell the houses or if it commemorates the street light in the foreground. The concrete pole, light globe, and the clouds overhead have been inserted into the picture.

Street lights were a selling point, since the county did not require street lighting when the houses were built. The parks, the shopping center, and the nine-foot-wide panels of grass and trees dividing residential streets from cross-town traffic weren't required either.

87

Drive from the ocean to Los Angeles, and you'll stay on the same grid of streets. The drive passes through suburb after suburb without interruption.

It is a distance of fifteen miles, over land so worthless a hundred years ago that house lots on it could not be given away.

What later redeemed the land—and determined its limits—are the subdivision maps filed in the county recorder's office.

88

Every map is a fiction. Every map offers choices.
It's even possible to choose something beautiful.

89

For this photograph my father sat on the lawn of his house playing with my brother. Behind him, the wood railing of the porch was unobscured by the pyracantha bushes.

Over the years, the pyracanthas swelled out of the limits of the garden.

Both my parents are dead; my older brother moved away to repair cars. I live in the house that belonged to the three of them, the house my parents bought for $6,700, and into which my brother was born as their first gift.

I have taken their places, displacing everything of theirs except the way in which they succeeded in fitting into this small house before I was born.

My brother and I, who shared a room for almost twenty years, slept in identical beds. Our bedspreads were always the same.

We slept east to west in our room and less than fourteen feet from our parents, in their bedroom at the front of the house.

Only once did I hear their lovemaking, although I was a fitful sleeper and lay awake hours every night looking up at the ceiling, imagining other houses in which to live.

Now I sleep better in this house, and I am grateful.

90

After work at city hall, I walk home on straight, flat side-walks. Their lines converge ahead of me into a confusion of trees and lawns.

The sidewalk is four feet wide. The street is forty feet wide. The strip of lawn between the street and the sidewalk is seven feet. The setback from curb to house is twenty feet.

This pattern—of asphalt, grass, concrete, grass—is as regular as any thought of God's.

91

It is not simply missed opportunities that leave him the humiliation of his comfortable house and his regular habits. The opportunities, themselves, appear out of place.

He prayed at first to be relieved of his life, and not to know when his prayer would be answered. When it was, he prayed for other people's plans.

92

I learned about one of the thirty-two names on the city's Vietnam memorial plaque. All I learned was that the name belonged to the son of a machinist.

Even as an old man, in the 1980s, the machinist rode his motorcycle to work on the night shift at Douglas Aircraft. I spoke to him two or three times a year, but not about his son who had died in Vietnam.

The old man continued to coach at the park near his house. He volunteered for twenty years to teach eight- and nine-year-old boys how to play baseball.

Park sports have been coached by volunteers in my city since 1956. The coaches are often the sons, even the grandsons, of the first volunteers.

Each year before he died, the machinist gave me $100 in cash to buy tickets to the city's annual sports banquet for any coach or player who could not afford to go.

93

The question really was, who could be trusted to buy these small houses? Characteristically, the developers did not bother answering it.

The subdivision's sales manager said in 1951, "We sell happiness in homes."

His salesmen sold 30 to 50 houses a day, and more than 300 during one weekend, when the first unit of the subdivision opened. At one point, salesmen sold 107 houses in an hour.

They sold 7,400 houses in less than ten months.

Buyers only needed a steady job and the promise they would keep up the payments.

94

Sheetrock panels cover the interior walls of my house. Paint covers the plastered sheetrock. The walls have been painted white for more than thirty years.

When my mother left the house to die in the hospital nearby, congestive heart failure had swelled her legs and feet, and made her clumsy. She sat on the edge of her bed and could not dress herself on the day she left.

My father was outside, readying the car. I waited in the hallway, at the doorway to my room.

At the last moment, she found a new fear. "Don't come in," she said to me. "I'm not covered."

She called out to my father, who came to the front door. "He can't come in, he would see me," she said to him.

My father came back inside to help her dress in a clean nightgown and to keep from me the sight of my mother. I was thirty-one.

After my father died, I had the rooms painted white again.

95

His religion and living in this suburb have taught him shame.

It is a lesson he takes on his daily walk to work. He passes the houses of people he does not know, though he has lived on his block for forty-six years.

His walk into the center of the city is a little more than a mile.

96

The San Gabriel River crosses my city. The river channel is completely lined in concrete against a repetition of the disastrous floods of the 1930s.

Set in the floor of the San Gabriel River is a smaller concrete slot, a miniature river that flows constantly with a foot or two of water discharged from the county's waste water treatment plant.

Only when it rains is there more water in the San Gabriel River than this shallow band about a dozen feet wide.

At night, in the reflection of hundreds of street lamps, the substitute river glows.

97

A middle-aged man drove north on a Sunday night in January from an apartment in Orange County. He had his choice of freeway off-ramps; he chose one that brought him to my city.

He stopped where streets end at the San Gabriel River, and where the city had expanded a neighborhood park.

He crossed several hundred feet of the park's newly planted turf to climb an Edison Company transmission tower.

The legs of these towers, starting ten feet off the ground and for a height of another dozen feet, are faced with steel sawtooth strips. Each tooth is a blade, two or three inches long. Each strip of blades is longer than a man's reach.

There are no fences around the transmission towers. There is no need.

The man climbed one of the towers. He pulled himself, hand over hand, over the steel strips.

When he reached the top, he was pierced and bleeding.

The man saw the grid of houses laid out in lights. He saw the interlace of the roads, the interruption of the river, and its band of glowing water.

It was a clear night. The man reached up.

98

With state and federal grants, the city built a park under the power lines, since no houses can be built under the wires.

The city built jogging paths, playgrounds, picnic shelters, and restrooms. The city planted a meadow of California wildflowers around the base of one of the transmission towers.

The park improvements are modest, but modern and adequate. Mothers bring their children and push strollers along the mile of concrete jogging paths.

When the park was completed, the city council named it

in honor of a retiring city council member. She had been an original incorporator of the city in 1954 and then a park commissioner.

More than two thousand people turned out to see the park dedicated in the councilwoman's honor, and to eat a free pancake breakfast.

99

The park also is an equestrian center. The horses boarded there turned in their stalls at the flash of light and a sound like thunder.

Nothing more happened. No one in the houses nearby called the sheriff's station next to city hall for help.

Help for what?

A jogger's dog on Monday afternoon found the man, a black bundle in the grass the landscape superintendent leaves deliberately tall in the park's wildflower meadow.

100

The suicide was first reported as a murder—a man had been stabbed to death, his body dumped into the city's wildflowers, and the body set on fire.

Sheriff's investigators said it was a murder for revenge.

Later, they said the man had murdered his stepdaughter. He strangled her. Then he killed his wife, beating her until her face was unrecognizable.

Then he got into his car and began to drive.

101

The development of the city bypassed the two-hundred-foot-wide corridors of the Edison transmission towers.

Recently, the company began encouraging use of its rights of way. They have become parks, the city's community garden, wholesale plant nurseries, and truck farms.

There are now only a few empty commercial lots in the city. Out of nine-and-a-half square miles, the unbuilt area is about thirty acres.

Every square foot of my city has been tilled or built on and fitted into the grid.

102

I work late at city hall, and I walk home in the dark. Sometimes I work late on Sunday.

At 10 p.m. on Sunday, walking home on the sidewalk bordering the access road designed to separate the highway from residential streets, I was stopped.

A car slowed and pulled up to the curb at the corner of my block. I turned and walked toward it automatically. I am always asked directions, because I am almost always the only pedestrian.

A young man quickly stepped from the car. He pointed a gun at my chest and asked for my wallet.

I said, "I'm sorry, I don't understand you."

As I said this, I decided to fall backward onto the lawn of

the corner house. As I fell, I may have looked like someone who had just been shot.

Nothing else happened. The porch light of the house behind me came on. I heard the door of the car close; I heard the car drive away.

I lay still for a few moments longer, looking up at the stars in the clear sky through the limbs of a leafless jacaranda tree.

103

Jacarandas bloom in early May, before the new leaves show. The horn-shaped flowers are the color of the sky at late dusk—a pure, translucent purple.

That color is held overhead on the thin branches of the tree's new growth. Thousands of small flowers fall soon after blooming, covering the sidewalk and lawn with purple in a fifty-foot circle.

None of the city's trees are as exotic as the jacarandas, which are native to the Amazon basin.

There were no trees here when the land was farmed, except a stand of eucalyptus planted near the field office of the Montana Land Company. These trees now shade the water department office and the city's print shop.

Eucalyptus trees are native to Australia.

By ordinance, every house must have a city tree planted in front of it. The tree is planted in the rectangle of land, seven feet wide and thirty feet long, which is the city's right of way in front of each house.

None of the city's street trees is native to California.

104

A Mexican family sits in the dense shade of a parkway tree—a *Ficus benjamina*—on the front lawn of the corner house.

The corner is on Hedda Street, named for Hedda Hopper. Several streets in the part of town where I live are named for radio and Hollywood personalities of the 1940s.

Two streets nearby intersect as Amos and Andy.

The family is waiting for a Long Beach bus that will stop a hundred feet farther on, in the sun. While they wait, two school-age girls play quietly.

Their father lies on his side in the shade and leans on his arm. He wears a traditional straw hat from his state in Mexico. The hat has a narrow brim and a bright, yarn band.

The woman sits bolt upright on the grass, in a loose dress, staring in the direction the bus will come, her legs wide in an open V.

No one in my neighborhood ever sits on the front lawn.

105

The National Arbor Day Foundation has named us a Tree City for the past six years. The award commends the city for maintaining its street trees and replacing those that die. This is called urban forestry.

Some residents, however, make other arrangements. They dislike trees, or what they drop, or the shade on their lawn.

They girdle their tree to kill it, or pound a ring of copper nails into the trunk to poison it, or cut it down themselves.

When the city replaces the tree, some of these residents kill it again.

The tree belongs to the city, and each new, fifteen-gallon replacement costs about $70 to plant. The city will replant a tree twice more.

After three replants, the city's right of way is left empty.

106

I work in my front yard on Saturday mornings.

My front yard is fifty feet wide and thirty-five feet deep. It includes the seven-foot-wide parkway strip that is the city's right of way.

The parkway is planted with a small crape myrtle tree that flowers red in spring. There is a maple tree in the front lawn. Two birch trees flank the front porch.

When I look up from my garden, two rows of mature Brazilian peppertrees converge in the distance.

The trees have dark trunks and small, dark-green leaves. In season, they litter the sidewalk with pink peppercorns.

The city no longer plants this variety of tree.

In 1979, a few days after my mother's funeral, the Brazilian peppertree in front of my house split from age and drought. The city replaced the tree a few years later with a red crape myrtle.

The rest of the street will be replanted with new trees when the city can afford them.

107

The forty-year-old Brazilian peppertrees aren't tall, but they have spreading crowns that extend over the sidewalk and the street. The city trims the trees every few years to keep facing pairs from arching over the narrow street.

Trimming the trees isn't for aesthetic reasons. Trimming clears access for the city's trash trucks.

Some houses on my street have a tree planted in the front lawn. Most houses have at least one tree in the backyard. Most of the trees are thirty or forty years old. Some of the trees tower over the houses.

Aerial photographs of this suburb from 1950 and 1951 are reprinted in textbooks on urban design and landscaping.

The photographs show rows of light-colored houses in a treeless waste.

108

I have a yard service mow my lawn twice a month. I replant my front garden twice a year, with spring and winter annuals.

Most of my neighbors do the same, though not all.

No one spends much time in their front yard, except the young husbands and wives of new families. They mow and edge their own lawns.

The city does not compel owners to mow their lawns regularly. But if they don't, their neighbors complain to city hall.

Beginning in the 1850s in America, city planners and architects sought to domesticate the condition of working people by setting their houses in a landscape.

The houses of working people would have a lawn and garden, to soften the view.

The houses would be small, because extended families would no longer live in them.

The small houses would be affordable, so that even a machinist could buy one.

Living in them would, however, require orderly lives.

When I walk to work, I walk through a vista that is almost one continuous garden and lawn, broken every fifty feet by a concrete driveway.

109

The afternoon of the day my father died, the shadows of eucalyptus trees planted by the city lay across the boulevards that border my neighborhood.

That August day was part of a very long youth. It was not a better time. I would not live it again.

110

The bank auctioned off Mr. H's house, after disclosing that it needed repairs. The bank thought the property would sell for little more than the value of its loan.

The bids went well above the $119,000 minimum. The successful bidder thought Mr. H's house was worth the much higher price.

A few days after the auction, the new owner and a city building inspector met at the house.

They found, among other things, that Mr. H had excavated a room beneath his garage. The room is nearly three hundred square feet and deep enough for a man to stand in comfortably.

Mr. H had dug a fallout shelter.

He tunneled under the floor of the garage, lined the empty space with rows of old water heaters filled with concrete, and braced the garage floor with railroad ties.

A metal hatch lets down into the underground room.

The concrete slab of the garage floor spans the excavation. The city inspector believes that the garage floor will collapse if a car is driven on it.

The new owner of the house is angry. He should never have bought the house, he says.

He doesn't know how much it will cost to bring the house into compliance with the city's building ordinances.

111

You and I were trained for a conflict that never came.

At my grade school, the Sisters of St. Joseph made me hate Communists, then intolerance, and finally everything that could break the charmed pattern of our lives.

I am not sure the Sisters of St. Joseph expected this from their daily lessons on the Red threat.

112

The nuns' stories made me want to keep everything that I could. First, I would keep my faith.

Much later, I would keep our regard for each other, and the ways in which we revealed ourselves in these small houses.

113

A loss of belief is what separates us from the much-handled things we grew up with.

114

My father and I returned to our house from my mother's funeral, and I never spoke to him of her again.

Once, shortly before my father's death, he broke down in tears and said, "You and your brother never talk about her."

Still, I would say nothing to him.

115

My father's life seemed to be about this: It was necessary to choose, but only once.

Every choice limited God's choices, and cut you off forever from other graces.

116

I cannot tell you what I care for. I can only tell you what I fear to lose.

117

Three businessmen arranged to buy the Montana Land Company in 1949.

With $8.9 million in borrowed money, they bought the company's stock and ten square miles of indifferent Southern California farmland on the outskirts of Long Beach.

The sale included the empty lots—70 feet wide by 120 feet long—in a residential subdivision the Montana Land Company had laid out in 1929. The company's dead-level acres of former sugar beet fields surrounded a golf course.

The Montana Land Company had hoped to sell the land as house lots. To lure middle-class buyers from Long Beach, about six miles away, the company first built the golf course. It was 175 acres of what had been a river bed.

In 1978, I wrote a history of the suburb the three businessmen built on the mostly empty land they bought. The suburb had become a city, and city officials had the history printed for students to use in school projects. Boy Scouts still use it to earn a merit badge for citizenship.

Clark J. Bonner had managed the Montana Land Company for the Clark family members who owned it. He planned the golf course and the residential streets in a subdivision that curved around an artificial lake.

I interviewed Clark Bonner's son when I began writing the city's history.

He told me, "And then, my father sold the land to those three Jews."

118

Louis Boyar, Mark Taper, and Ben Weingart built the city I live in and where I work. The three men built 17,500 houses in less than three years.

Time magazine said in 1950 that it was the biggest housing development in the world.

The three men bought the land with a loan from the Prudential Insurance Company, and began building the houses with money from an investment syndicate.

The Federal Housing Authority put up more than $100 million in construction loans and mortgage guarantees.

With more of Prudential's money, Weingart began building one of the nation's most successful suburban shopping centers. It was three times as large as the Northgate shopping center, which opened in 1950 outside Seattle.

Weingart's shopping center was a model for suburban retailing for the next thirty years. Thousands of duplicate shopping centers repeated its level acres of parking lots, pedestrian mall, and the three-hundred-foot setback that separates stores from the highway.

That three-hundred-foot distance is what separates a shopping center from Main Street.

119

Ben Weingart grew up a Christian Scientist.

His father died in 1892. His mother gave him up, at the age of four, to an orphanage in Atlanta.

When he was six, the orphanage loaned him out to pick cotton. A Christian Scientist woman saw him and unofficially adopted him.

The woman had a granddaughter crippled by polio. The boy was useful in looking after the girl.

The three of them were a family, although the boy kept his parents' name—Weingarten. He turned this later into Weingart.

The woman's name was Miller.

120

William A. Clark was one of the ten richest men in America. He owned the United Verde copper mine in Arizona and silver mines in Montana. He had been an architect of Montana statehood.

In 1899, Clark offered to bring Los Angeles another transcontinental railroad connection. The new line wouldn't be part of any railroad trust. It would lower the rates for freight, and force the Union Pacific to do the same.

City officials in Los Angeles gave Clark the franchise to build a thousand-mile rail line from the city's port at San Pedro to the Salt Lake City terminus of the Union Pacific.

The tracks of Clark's Terminal Railroad actually went from San Pedro to Pasadena, a distance of about forty miles.

Clark sold the railroad to the Union Pacific.

Clark's brother was made a member of the Union Pacific's board of directors.

In 1901, Clark bought the Montana state legislature and became a United States Senator.

121

William A. Clark began buying farmland in Southern California and invested in a sugar mill in Los Alamitos in Orange County. There was money to be made in sugar beets. The government supported domestic production with a protective tariff of 76 percent.

In 1904, Clark organized his Southern California holdings as the Montana Land Company with his brother, J.

Ross Clark. Later, they made Clark Bonner, J. Ross Clark's nephew, president of the company.

William A. Clark died in 1925 and left an estate worth $200 million.

In 1926, Clark Bonner closed the sugar mill and leased the company's former beet fields to tenant farmers.

In 1929, Clark Bonner began subdividing the company's farmland.

The Depression and the Second World War followed.

122

According to Mark Taper, the stockholders arranged to sell the Montana Land Company because postwar corporate taxes were 77 percent. It wasn't profitable, he said, for the company to subdivide its land in small tracts to real estate developers.

According to his son, Bonner was frustrated by so many acres without landmarks.

123

The sale of the Montana Land Company included all the remaining lots in the middle-class subdivision Clark Bonner laid out in 1929. The sale also included the company-run golf course, which Bonner had intended to be an exclusive country club.

In the late 1940s, the doctors, college professors, and retired naval officers who lived in the houses east of the golf course still called it "the country club." It had never been one; it has always been a public golf course.

The property owners in Bonner's subdivision reacted

immediately to the sale of the Montana Land Company and the golf course. They were afraid the three developers planned to subdivide the course into more lots for thousand-square-foot tract houses.

They knew who would live in them.

The three developers needed the cooperation of the county to build 17,500 houses in thirty-three months. The three men quickly leased the golf course to the county.

124

Near the first tee at the golf course is a memorial to Clark Bonner.

County Supervisor Herbert Legg suggested the memorial on the day the three developers were forced to lease the golf course to the county.

The memorial is a bronze plaque, originally paid for by the members of the Chamber of Commerce. When county workers removed the plaque and lost it many years later, Bonner's son bought a new plaque and replaced it.

The plaque is mounted on the side of a platform built of tan Palo Verde stone. An olive tree grows in the center of the platform.

The monument used to include a drinking fountain and a bench for golfers coming off the front nine holes. The county recently took these out and replaced Bonner's plaque.

On the new plaque, the bronze letters that spell out the name of the county supervisor for this district are as big as those that spell Bonner's name.

The monument—with its olive tree and revised commemorative plaque—interrupts the short walk to the next tee.

The plaque says that Clark Bonner founded my city.

125

Ben Weingart arranged the financing to buy the Montana Land Company.

He persuaded Investor's Diversified Services, an investment syndicate based in Minneapolis, and the Prudential Insurance Company to underwrite $250 million in mortgages. He persuaded the insurance company to invest another $8 million to build the shopping center.

Weingart and Louis Boyar risked $15,000 of their own money to form the corporation that built the houses. Boyar was the president of the corporation.

Mark Taper was born in Poland and raised in England. He had made a fortune in the 1930s, building the row houses being put up by the British government. He retired to California in 1939, far from the war in Europe.

Taper was the vice president of the corporation. He invested no money of his own in the partnership that built the houses.

In 1954, Taper retired from construction a second time to operate a savings and loan he had bought in 1950. Its depositors financed new subdivisions and shopping centers, but not in the suburb Taper had built.

In 1980, Taper sold American Savings for $200 million.

126

Ben Weingart left school in the third grade. The family he lived with left Georgia for Detroit when he was ten. He left them when he was fifteen.

He worked as a delivery boy, then as a route laundryman

for brothels in St. Louis. By the time he was seventeen he was working a confidence game with a traveling eye doctor selling nearly worthless glasses in the Midwest.

He arrived in Los Angeles in 1906, when he was eighteen. He got another job delivering laundry. Later, he bought the business.

Weingart impressed Morgan Adams, a Los Angeles real estate promoter who owned hotels on Weingart's laundry route. He asked Weingart to manage some of them. Before he was twenty-seven, Weingart owned one himself.

Weingart mortgaged the hotel, borrowed, and bought more hotels in downtown Los Angeles. He borrowed enough to lose real estate investments worth $20 million in 1929.

He managed to hold on to some of his property, including the El Rey, a hotel favored by prostitutes.

127

Long Beach boomed in the 1920s. There was oil under the city's harbor and even more under new suburban housing tracts on Signal Hill. By 1929, the open land on the outskirts of Long Beach was covered with hundred-foot-tall wood derricks.

The Clark family's fields of sugar beets were outside the oil field by less than a mile.

Clark Bonner persuaded the Clarks that they still could make money from the boom. He recommended subdividing the company's land into industrial tracts and residential neighborhoods.

In his plan, manufacturing plants would go next to a spur of the railroad William A. Clark had sold.

Houses would go where two country roads crossed at right angles.

Residential streets would curve around a golf course, a stand of eucalyptus trees, and an artificial lake that had begun as a tourist attraction created by a spectacular artesian well.

Bonner wanted to build a village of middle-class houses in the popular Spanish Colonial style. The houses, like the golf course clubhouse, would have pink stucco walls and red tile roofs.

Bonner named the subdivision after a 19th-century New Jersey resort town where John D. Rockefeller had once spent his summers.

128

When it began, Los Angeles had no riverfront, harbor, or highway to somewhere else more important.

Before Colonel de Neve opened his notebook and drew a plan showing house lots around a plaza and the church, Los Angeles had no explanation.

129

Los Angeles was founded by royal order in 1781. The principal reason for its location was its distance from the San Gabriel Mission, about ten miles away.

The priests insisted on the separation. They feared the effect of the secular town on their Native American converts.

Long Beach was settled in 1881 by a handful of like-minded teetotalers and evangelicals. They, too, insisted on distances.

During the real estate boom of 1887, a dozen cities in Los Angeles County were sketched into the white spaces on United States Geologic Survey maps.

Most of the speculative cities began with a water company, a railroad siding, and a wood-frame hotel.

Sometimes, there wasn't the railroad siding. Sometimes the water company had no water.

There was, however, always a subdivision map.

It showed potential buyers where a downtown of banks and commercial blocks would be built, where public libraries would be founded, and where rectangular lots would stretch out into empty fields.

130

The railroads profited from the square miles of California land the federal government gave them as construction bounty. Their surveyors laid the grid for square "railroad towns" beside the rails.

The railroad surveyors repeated the pattern of right angles over and over because it was familiar and cheap.

131

The golf course and clubhouse—opened shortly after the repeal of Prohibition in 1933—were supposed to make it easier to sell house lots.

Clark Bonner also persuaded the Long Beach Unified School District to build a two-year college at the center of the new subdivision. He persuaded the members of the school board by giving them the thirty acres of land they needed.

The college, which opened in 1935, is in Spanish Colonial's massive public style. Poured concrete stands in for adobe.

In 1937, Bonner's subdivision had just twenty-seven houses. A few of them had pink stucco walls and red tile roofs.

132

Clark Bonner contracted with the Janss Company to develop the new subdivision in 1929. The Janss Company had developed Westwood, among other Los Angeles-area communities.

The large lots on three curving streets didn't sell.

Bonner contracted with Charles Hopper, the developer of Bel-Air and South Gate. In 1934, Hopper began advertising "semi-sustaining garden homes" on lots that were 120 feet wide and 150 feet long.

"Semi-sustaining" meant that property owners could keep enough chickens to make egg money. They could keep a kitchen garden and can the produce.

There was a depression on. The streets in the redesigned subdivision didn't curve.

Still, in the sales brochure for Bonner's subdivision, young women on horseback smiled. A stucco house with a tile roof showed the taste of those who purchased lots. A gas station, photographed against an absolutely featureless waste, showed that the community was up to date.

The golf course clubhouse was called *La Casa de Buenos Amigos*—The House of Good Friends.

133

Emile Kosa, the noted California artist, painted two murals for the patio of the clubhouse.

They were reproduced on the clubhouse menu.

The two murals are impressions of pre-Yankee California—the sort of picture once called "romance of the ranchos."

The first is a market scene. A señorita carries a basket of tropical fruit on her head. Three mariachi musicians play in the street. A man rides on a donkey. The sky is clear and brilliant.

The second mural shows a bull ring. A toreador, waiting to fight his bull, stands in front of a group of men squatting on the ground. Their sombreros make wide shadows. One man is sleeping in the shade of a palm tree.

A few men, hands in their pockets, watch the bullfight indifferently.

The two murals are gone, either painted over when the clubhouse patio was enclosed in the 1940s, or removed when the golf course was sold to the three developers.

134

In 1950, *Time* magazine described the construction of the first unit of the 17,500 houses going up on what had been the Clarks' bean fields.

Time described one of the developers, Louis Boyar, as "swarthy" and "shy." The meaning of "swarthy" was clear. It ended any speculation whether Boyar was a Jew.

When the three developers bought the Montana Land Company's empty fields, the sale included the remaining house lots around the company's golf course.

In the 1930s and 1940s, the Montana Land Company made it very clear in its promotional material that the lots were protected by "restrictions of an all-inclusive nature." Written into deed covenants, these restrictions prevented the sale of lots to Negroes, Mexicans, and Jews.

In 1948, the Supreme Court made racial restrictions in property ownership unenforceable, but covenants—including those against Jews—continued to be written into deeds in Long Beach.

Neighboring property owners could still sue for lowering property values if a seller violated the unenforceable racial restrictions.

In 1953, the Supreme Court made homeowner lawsuits to enforce racial covenants unconstitutional.

135

Louis Boyar, Mark Taper, and Ben Weingart bought Clark Bonner's speculative subdivision in 1949.

It was a suburb in which they could not live.

136

Clark Bonner had built just three of the curving streets in the subdivision he planned. The streets faced the putting green of the first hole of his golf course.

Bonner had sold real estate developers another four thousand lots that were much more modest, including the neighborhood where I live.

Perhaps Bonner's disappointing housing tracts could be dismissed, if they were sold to the three Jews.

Thirty years later, Bonner's son seemed to say that anyone who would live in the town those men had built was welcome to it.

It was often said of this suburb, as its houses filled quickly in 1950 and 1951, that every other house was either Jewish or Catholic.

I lived in one of the houses that was Catholic.

137

This suburb still has many Catholic families. It has fewer Jewish ones.

A subsidiary of Chevron Oil is building the city's last subdivision. The thirty-three acres, on the city's west side, will yield about 185 houses, some with floor plans that have four and five bedrooms.

Many of the families buying these houses—which cost about $350,000—are likely to be Catholic.

The tract is in a small, mostly Hispanic school district with a reputation for gangs.

The tract of new houses is across the street from the city's Catholic church and its elementary school. A Catholic girls' high school and a boys' high school are not far away.

138

In Levittown on Long Island in 1953, for reasons no one in the Levitt organization explained, the population of new homeowners was 50 percent Catholic.

139

My grandmother wrote to my father in 1937 that her seven sons were candle flames that should be lost in the greater light of Christ.

Her sons met part of that obligation.

Uncle Frank was a lawyer. My grandmother hoped that he would, like some Counter-Reformation saint, be both lawyer and priest. He didn't. He died not long after his marriage at fifty-seven.

Uncle Tom joined the Fathers of the Blessed Sacrament,

but became an Army chaplain. He served in the Second World War, Korea, and Vietnam. He was an Army skydiver when he retired. He went back to his religious congregation reluctantly.

Uncle Jack became a Maryknoll missionary among the Quechua in the highlands of Peru. Later, he became an alcoholic. He married, was divorced, and died in West Virginia.

Uncle George became a parish priest to working-class Catholics in Louisville, Kentucky. He retired there.

Uncle Ken married, had three daughters and two sons, and sold insurance in Pittsburgh. He died on his front porch of a heart attack the week my father died.

Uncle Arthur has a small business in Maryland.

140

Joe Eichenbaum's daughter married Louis Boyar's son in 1948. Eichenbaum met Ben Weingart at the wedding reception.

He told Weingart that he had managed two small department stores in Chicago before retiring with his wife to California.

Weingart offered to make Eichenbaum a partner in his company if he would manage the building and leasing of the new shopping center Weingart was going to build.

Eichenbaum was skeptical of the design when he saw it.

He knew that one of the first suburban shopping centers

set back from the street had been built in Framingham, Massachusetts only a year before.

It had gone bankrupt.

141

Joe Eichenbaum thought that setting store windows back from the street contributed to the failure of the shopping center in Framingham.

Few retailers before 1950 had successfully turned away from the street, where they thought shoppers, pushing in crowds on the sidewalk, made an impulsive choice to buy.

Weingart persuaded Eichenbaum that the habits of shoppers could be changed by the places in which they shopped. Eichenbaum persuaded the May family to gamble on a store that had only a few small show windows barely visible from the boulevard, three hundred feet away.

142

The May Co. department store was the principal anchor store in the shopping center Ben Weingart built.

Weingart got Prudential Insurance to invest $8 million in the shopping center by first getting the May Co. to agree to build a store.

He signed a sweetheart lease with the May Company in 1951, a year after the first houses had been sold.

Provisions in the May Co. lease kept other major department stores out of the shopping center for almost twenty years.

143

The May Co. sold everything needed to make a home when the store opened in February 1952. It sold china, violins, permanent waves, and washing machines.

The store was designed in the International Style by

Albert C. Martin Associates. The building cost $11 million. It was as nearly perfect as an almost featureless building can be.

It was a 357,000-square-foot, three-story, rectangular box of white concrete.

Above the building—the highest point of the city for many years—were the emblems of the May Co. They were four letter Ms, each facing a cardinal point of the compass.

144

The May Co. building was topped with a windowless white cube that concealed elevator and air-conditioning machinery. This supported the four letters that soon identified the entire shopping center.

When the store opened, the four letters could be seen from every street in the new suburb. Each letter M was sixteen feet high.

It was announced in the local paper that the letters could be seen from sixty miles away in some directions, and that the letters would help guide aircraft.

At night, the letters lighted inside by neon tubes, glowed a bright yellow.

145

Joe Eichenbaum negotiated the deals for Ben Weingart's new shopping center.

He calculated the mall's carrying capacity of shoe stores, jewelry stores, and chain clothing stores. He decided which stores went in, as he leased vacant retail spaces in 1951 and 1952.

Shoe stores were important, but not for shoes.

Banks were uncertain about the shopping center's future. They financed other retailers only if Eichenbaum showed that major chain stores—shoe stores mainly—had signed long-term leases.

The more shoe stores Eichenbaum leased, the more financing his other retailers found.

Eichenbaum made these rules up as he went along.

146

The shopping center grew to cover 264 acres, although most of this is a parking lot. The center had parking for 10,580 cars in 1954. By 1980, it had parking for 12,000.

The parking spaces, striped in white on the new asphalt, were nine feet wide so that opening a car door wouldn't scratch the paint on a neighboring car.

Because of the size of the parking lots, it was the largest shopping center in the world. That fact is still mentioned when city officials are asked to describe the city.

The shopping center is no longer the world's largest.

147

In 1952, a magazine for grade school students told the story of the new suburb. The story is illustrated with an aerial photograph.

The photograph shows the shopping center as a square with half-mile-long sides surrounded by rows of houses.

The caption of the photograph says the tracts of houses surround a defense plant.

148

The shopping center was going to have office buildings, a hospital, a post office, a motel, county government offices, and a bowling alley.

There were to be ninety stores along a pedestrian mall that was eighteen hundred feet long. The May Co. and the smaller Butler Brothers department store, opened three months earlier, anchored the northern section in 1952.

A tunnel half a mile long connected the basements of the stores. There were no loading docks at ground level for any of the stores. No delivery trucks or cross streets interrupted shoppers as they walked.

It was an open-air mall. Fifteen-foot overhangs shaded a sixty-foot walkway between the two rows of stores.

The mall was semitropically landscaped. Raised planters held ferns, palms, and bird-of-paradise plants. There were concrete benches built into the planters for tired mothers to sit with impatient children.

Decorations were installed to indicate the seasons.

Hidden ten-inch RCA loudspeakers attached to light standards played continuous music. During the Christmas holidays, the loudspeakers played traditional carols.

Originally, the loudspeakers were supposed to broadcast the descriptions of lost children.

149

As soon as the shopping center opened in 1952, the half-mile-long service tunnel beneath the stores was designated a Civil Defense fallout shelter.

The first Soviet atomic bomb had been tested in August 1949.

Fallout shelters were marked by yellow and black metal signs with three white triangles.

The shelter signs went up at both ends of the tunnel, on nine-foot-high, galvanized steel poles.

Joe Eichenbaum's publicist noted in press releases that the tunnel had space enough to shelter thousands in the event of a nuclear war.

150

When Long Beach tried to annex the suburb he had helped build, Ben Weingart considered incorporating the shopping center and a strip of houses around it as a city.

Under California law, five hundred residents can make a city.

151

Major department stores still anchor successful shopping centers.

Department stores help define the shopping center's contours and its customers.

The anchor department stores distribute access to the big retailers of shoes and women's clothing that flank them. The anchors create foot traffic for the specialty stores that fill the spaces in between.

Too few anchors, too far apart, and the chain stores and specialty stores fail.

Anchor department stores get favorable leases. The major chain stores make less attractive deals.

Specialty retailers pay a premium to keep their place. They often pay a higher percentage of gross sales in lease payments and common-area fees.

Specialty stores in shopping malls frequently fail. They are expected to.

The owners of the mall calculate at least a ten percent turnover in leases every year. The turnover is designed to keep shoppers interested.

152

The letters on top of the May Co. did not conform to the city's sign ordinance, which requires that signs name something. The letters were removed in 1982, the year my father died.

The letters were the only graceful part of the building.

153

My father often said that he was a simple man. I do not believe my father was, but I admired his claim.

I admired my father's grace as well, which made him angry.

154

There were some graces my father rejected. He accepted the ones that let him live his life here.

155

The master plan for the subdivision specified an ornamental tree in front of each house in the city's right-of-way. Each house was provided with a small fifteen-gallon tree in the space between the sidewalk and the curb.

Every block had its own variety of tree. The trees were chosen for their low cost and quick growth.

When they were newly planted, the trees were too small to hide the May Co. building or the capital Ms that were its emblem.

The trees have now reached their full height. Many have begun to die.

The roots of the most aggressive trees buckle sidewalks and break up curbs. Residents complain, mostly about the ponding water that tree roots trap on the city's flat streets.

The city will remove many of its thirty thousand street trees in the next twenty years. Removal and replanting will cost the city more than two million dollars.

You rarely notice the May Co. building. It's hidden by the crowns of mature trees in every direction.

156

On Memorial Day in 1967, the city dedicated a plaque to its men killed in Vietnam. The new plaque, bolted to the *Skynight*'s concrete pylon, had two names on it.

There was room, however, to fit thirty-eight more, on six-inch strips of cast bronze.

For the next five years, the city ordered new names for Memorial Day. The names were taken from newspaper obituaries and at the request of parents or grandparents. A city worker attached the new bronze strips to the plaque with aluminum rivets.

The sons of the veterans of the Second World War and the Korean War came of age together. I was one of them.

The draft took the unlucky when college deferments ran out; enlistment took those who were patriotic or rebellious.

By 1973 there were thirty-two names on the city's plaque.

157

Because new names were added to the plaque each year, every Memorial Day between 1967 and 1973 included unveiling the plaque and reading all the names again.

By 1977, when I began to work for the city, the reason for unveiling the plaque and reading the names was forgotten. There were no new names to add.

Each Memorial Day, city council members took down a black drape that covered the Vietnam plaque and read the names.

The audience of veterans and their wives had seen the city council members do the same for years.

158

The Vietnam plaque, with its names attached by aluminum rivets, was next to a playground. Sometimes, someone would pry a name off.

City council members, reading the names aloud during Memorial Day ceremonies, would notice the gap.

Later, the city's purchasing office would order a replacement. The list of names became increasingly inaccurate.

One name was missing for years. Another name was repeated. When council members read that name a second time on Memorial Day, they did not ask why one man was named twice.

Finally in 1982, I had the plaque taken down and replaced with one cast in solid bronze. The thirty-two names would not change.

One name is now permanently misspelled; another name is still missing.

City council members read them that way on Memorial Day.

159

Of those who have received the Medal of Honor since 1941, only 194 men are still living. Mr. C is not one of them. He never received the Medal of Honor.

He wears one, however, at meetings of the veterans' organizations to which he belongs.

He says he earned the Medal of Honor on his seventeenth birthday—on March 18, 1945—aboard the carrier

Franklin. He says he has a book with the whole story in it, which he cannot find among the stacks of war memorabilia that fill his house.

160

My job at city hall occasionally involves listening to the complaints of residents. The street light across from their house is burned out, or the city's parkway tree needs to be trimmed.

Before they complain, callers often begin by telling me how long they have lived here.

161

Some residents tell me the year they moved into their house because they think the city should take better care of original property owners.

Some tell me how long they have lived here because they think the city owes them something for persistence.

Most callers tell me out of habit.

162

A woman calls repeatedly about her Christmas tree.

The city's trash hauler picks up the discarded trees. If a tree is taller than four feet, it must be cut in half before the trash hauler will pick it up.

The woman's tree is over four feet. The woman has no one to saw her tree in two.

She is advised, gently, to ask a neighbor. But she won't.

She says she no longer knows her neighbors well
enough.

163

The developers subdivided the ten square miles they
bought into forty individual tracts. Most were 157 acres. A
few tracts were as small as 20 acres.

The biggest tracts had 640 houses each.

The families that moved into them averaged 4.2 persons,
higher than the national average of 3.2 in 1953. That
accounted for mom and dad and 2.2 children.

The biggest tracts had a population of 2,400 as soon as
the moving vans pulled away from the curb.

164

Families moved in at the rate of thirty-five a day. *Life* magazine recorded their arrival in a photo story.

Don Rochlen, the publicist for the developers, staged the
principal photograph. He offered local movers the chance
to have one of their trucks pictured in *Life.* The companies
provided more than a dozen moving vans.

Rochlen positioned a van in the driveway of nearly every
house along a block. He invited the homeowners who
wanted to be in *Life* to recreate their moving day.

Some brought a few chairs out of the house and set them
below the tailgate of the moving van in their driveway.

The *Life* photographer took the picture standing on top
of one of the vans.

The street, the moving vans, and the dwindling figures of
parents and children recede into the distance. The enor-

mous vans, their company names and telephone numbers painted on their sides, fill the foreground.

When you call the picture service for *Time* and *Life* and mention the name of my city, the archivist will ask if you want to purchase the staged photograph of the moving vans.

165

The *Life* story calculated the cost of moving into the new suburb.

The writer chose an average couple. He said they paid $10,290 for their house, including options. He said they spent another $6,860 for furnishings and a new car.

166

The engineering plan estimated that the completed development would have a population of about seventy thousand.

That was larger than the population of Tampa, Savannah, or South Bend.

167

At first, it wasn't a city at all.

The developers called it a "$250,000,000 planned community."

According to the engineering drawings, it was 105 acres of concrete sidewalks and 133 miles of paved streets lined with 5,000 concrete light poles. These were paid for by the three developers.

It was the service roads that paralleled the major streets, to keep traffic out of residential neighborhoods.

According to the sales brochure, it was two coats of paint on the interior walls and wallpaper above the chair rail in the dining room.

It was a garbage disposal in every kitchen. The sales brochure said the new suburb was "the only garbage-free city in the world."

It also was the developers' promise of twenty elementary schools, thirty-seven playgrounds, and eighteen churches. The sales brochure said the suburb would have "churches of every denomination." The brochure listed twenty-six.

The list of denominations is not alphabetized. Between *Presbyterian* and *Adventist* is listed *Synagogue.*

168

For nearly three years the pace of construction never slowed.

The governing board of one church was interested in a building site for a new parish. The board members made a tentative offer to the realty agent, but they had to wait for approval from their congregation.

When the congregation agreed to the price, the board members came back to buy the vacant property. They couldn't find it.

New houses already covered the site they had chosen for their church.

169

The Board of Supervisors in Los Angeles forced the three developers to lease their golf course to the county for $125,000 a year.

After negotiating the agreement, County Supervisor Herbert Legg suggested that Louis Boyar build a public swimming pool. Supervisor Legg thought the county's new pool should go next to the golf course clubhouse.

The residents around the clubhouse immediately objected. A public swimming pool would "impair play at the golf course."

Supervisor Legg suggested that Boyar build the pool in the county park near my house instead.

The pool cost Boyar's company $150,000 and the two acres of land under it.

The park at the edge of my neighborhood is called Mayfair Park. The nearby high school is Mayfair High.

Supervisor Legg suggested that the county's new pool in Mayfair Park be named in Boyar's honor. The Mayfair neighborhood association, however, refused to accept Boyar's name.

The pool is called Mayfair Pool.

170

In 1969, on the fifteenth anniversary of the city he had helped to build, Mark Taper recorded a conversation at city hall. He talked about the early days of my suburb with some of the other men who worked for the incorporation of the city.

The city clerk gave him a transcript of the conversation to correct.

Taper had spoken about Supervisor Herbert Legg and the $150,000 donation to build the county a swimming pool in Mayfair Park.

In making his corrections to the transcript, Taper crossed out the words *Legg insisted on $150,000* and wrote over them *Legg suggested*.

171

The corporation that built the houses and the shopping center dissolved after my suburb became a city in 1954.

The three developers divided the company's assets. Ben Weingart kept the shopping center. Joe Eichenbaum stayed on as manager. Eventually, he controlled the center's master leases.

Mark Taper got the golf course.

The new city attorney recommended that the county condemn Taper's property to keep the course intact when the county's lease ran out.

In 1969, after two months of condemnation proceedings in Superior Court, the county employee retirement fund paid $5,462,860 for Taper's golf course.

172

The critics of suburbs say that you and I live narrow lives.

I agree. My life is narrow.

From one perspective or another, all our lives are narrow. Only when lives are placed side by side do they seem larger.

173

Mrs. R and her husband lived across the street. They had a daughter, born a few months before my brother.

They were Episcopalians.

My mother and Mrs. R were friends. They spent afternoons in each other's houses, while my mother waited through her first pregnancy.

One afternoon, Mrs. R's baby stopped breathing. Mrs. R came to my mother's front door in tears, helpless.

Neither Mrs. R nor my mother had a car. Neither could drive. Few women in the neighborhood could.

It was 1946. Neither house had a telephone.

My mother, heavy with her baby, ran across the street into Mrs. R's house.

She picked up Mrs. R's daughter. She walked into the kitchen and turned on the faucet.

She cradled the dead baby in her arm against the curve of her stomach, and cupped her hand into the stream of water.

With a little of the water, she baptized the baby.

It was all she could do.

174

I saw my father cry only once before my mother's death. I was nine or ten.

It seemed to me that my parents were arguing about my father's health. I don't think they were. Something else had unfolded in their life together.

The argument stopped. My father came into the middle bedroom, where I had gone to be as far from them as I could. In this house, the greatest distance is fifteen or twenty feet.

My father sat on the end of the small bed that took the place of a couch in the middle room. The room was crowded with a desk, bookshelves my father built, the bed, and a black-and-white television set.

We sat a short distance from each other. My father cried.

The middle room became my bedroom when I entered college. I slept there on weekends when I went to graduate school in Orange County. It was my room when I left school and began a part-time teaching job.

After my mother died in 1979, my father suggested I take the larger, back bedroom.

I said no.

175

The greatest loss in living deliberately alone is in not having anyone to forgive.

176

My father brought his suitcase down from the attic after my mother's death, emptied it, and burned the letters he sent her during the war. He kept the letters my mother sent him.

He also kept the notebook he'd written in during his years as a member of a Catholic religious order.

I kept his notebook. I have not read it.

177

My father, although he did not prepare to become a priest, was a member of the Blessed Sacrament religious order from 1936 to early 1941.

Between 1942 and 1945, he was a gunnery officer aboard the USS *Bradford,* a destroyer in the Pacific.

After the war, he worked for the Southern California Gas Company. He wrote welding specifications for the pipelines that cross beneath the Los Angeles basin.

He designed pipelines for the Gas Company for thirty years.

178

I did not know why my father cried that afternoon, after arguing with my mother. Now, I think they were tears of humiliation.

179

The shopping center's designers calculated its psychological effects.

The designers said drivers will become subconsciously anxious when they see so many rows of parked cars.

The main parking lot at the shopping center slopes down from the May Co. toward the boulevard, three hundred feet away. The last row of parked cars before the highway is four feet lower than the street surface.

The designers put the acres of parking lot below the passing traffic, so that anxious drivers wouldn't see so many cars and miss the stores.

18O

Ben Weingart's shopping center was graded to stand out from the surrounding cars, the *Los Angeles Mirror* said, "like the screen in a drive-in movie theater."

181

The shopping center had more than one hundred acres of parking when it opened.

Joe Eichenbaum worried about the frustration of finding an empty parking space in so many acres of parked cars.

He proposed a system of towers and lights that would direct drivers.

A spotter on top of the May Co. building, and others in towers at either end of the mall, would activate a system of colored lights at the ends of the rows of parking spaces.

The colored lights would show drivers where they could park.

A control booth was put up on top of the May Co. building, but the rest of the system was never built.

182

Louis Boyar had faith in planning. He believed in a grid of streets meeting at right angles, and small houses centered on fifty-by-one-hundred-foot lots.

Boyar had drawn and redrawn this plan for a city while building houses in Long Beach in the late 1930s. Occasionally, when the work got slow, he sat down with a map and drew straight lines into the white space of the Montana Ranch.

He drew residential streets on the empty spaces in the grid laid out by Colonel de Neve, whose orders from the king of Spain specified house lots that were fifty-five feet wide by one hundred and ten feet deep.

183

The lots on Louis Boyar's design were slightly smaller than those required by the king of Spain.

Boyar's lots were fifty by one hundred feet, or five thousand square feet.

This was the minimum lot size allowed by Los Angeles County.

184

When places to live must be built quickly, cheaply, and profitably, they are built on a grid of right angles.

The neat rectangles of two-story, red brick barracks for political prisoners at Auschwitz—and the rows of wood sheds at the nearby Birkenau camp for the extermination of Jews—are built on a grid.

185

Birkenau means "Birch Wood."

The empty fields among the birch trees had once been farmland.

The men's camp at Birkenau, opposite a railroad siding, was almost a perfect square.

Inside, the wood sheds were separated by packed earth. Each one was on its own rectangular island, oriented precisely east and west.

Each shed was 36 feet wide and 116 feet long. Each had been built to house 550 prisoners.

When more space was required, the number of men in each shed was increased to 744.

Expansion did not require remodeling the structure. The men were simply packed closer together on the three tiers of square, wooden shelves on which they slept.

Oriented north and south on each shelf, four bodies could lie where three once had.

Other aspects of the camp's design were less efficient initially.

When spring thawed the waterlogged ground of Birkenau, frozen corpses rose to the surface.

186

Louis Boyar's wife told her husband to redesign the street plan he had sketched. She wanted him to add parkway panels and parallel service roads to separate the residential streets from highway traffic.

She told her husband that children like to play in the street, and how dangerous the streets were in Chicago where she grew up.

When construction began in 1950, the *Los Angeles Daily News* said the new community was "scientifically planned."

187

Louis Boyar took his engineering drawings to Los Angeles to meet with the county planning commission in 1950, shortly before the sale of the Montana Land Company was complete.

The commissioners met in the Hall of Administration, a

few hundred feet from where Colonel de Neve had opened
his notebook and begun to draw.

188

The planning commission was responsible for approving
Louis Boyar's subdivision plan.

The commissioners unrolled the thick bundle of blueprints that Boyar handed them. He pointed out the relevant
sections.

The first sheet of blueprints showed the street grid.
Beneath it lay more sheets with plans of water lines, sewer
laterals, and storm drains.

189

The county planning commission was not impressed with
the original design of Ben Weingart's shopping center.

The commissioners felt that a pedestrian shopping mall
surrounded by 10,580 parking spaces, each one nine feet
wide, would probably fail.

They allowed Weingart to build, but only on condition
that the subdivision's street grid break up the shopping
center's parking lots.

If the center went bankrupt, its acres of parking could be
subdivided for business lots without forcing the county to
pay for streets.

190

The commissioners were more impressed with another
design feature.

The intersections of the main streets in the new suburb, each one exactly a mile apart, were to be developed as neighborhood shopping centers.

There would be sixteen of them.

Each intersection would have a dry cleaner's, a barber and a beauty shop, and either a drug store or a small five-and-dime. Most intersections would have a grocery store.

The commissioners felt this was a practical design for the kind of city the three developers were building. The city was flat, and there were sidewalks everywhere.

In the early 1950s, housewives walked to the store, often two or three times a week, pushing babies in strollers or pulling older children in a red wagon behind them.

Forty years later, these neighborhood shopping centers are still no further than a half-mile from any house.

191

In 1953, a reporter for *Harper's Magazine* asked young wives living in my suburb what they missed most.

The women usually replied, "My mother."

192

I have a friend who grew up in the 1950s in the subdivision Clark Bonner planned.

He lived in a house on one of Charles Hopper's "semi-sustaining" lots, wide and deep enough for pole beans, an avocado tree, and a coop of chickens.

After the Second World War, not many households kept chickens.

My friend told me about his neighbors. They were Mexican. In the 1950s, that meant their parents—or even their grandparents—had originally come from Mexico.

The husband and his wife were dark-skinned. He was a pilot who flew tourists from Long Beach to Catalina Island, twenty-six miles away.

Before the pilot and his wife bought their house, the real estate agent told them about the racial restrictions in their deed.

The young couple told the real estate agent they were originally from Spain, not Mexico.

The real estate agent looked at the man and the woman, and signed the papers that sold them their house.

193

The subdivision Charles Hopper developed in 1934 didn't have sidewalks. The residents said that sidewalks weren't appropriate for their "garden suburb."

Some said they wouldn't want children roller skating or riding their bikes on the sidewalk in front of their house. Some said they didn't want to give up a narrow strip of their property for a public convenience.

In 1953, before the election that annexed these neighborhoods to Long Beach, Long Beach city officials said they would not require sidewalks.

By a majority of seventy-five votes, the residents of Clark Bonner's subdivision agreed to join the city of Long Beach.

The subdivision still doesn't have any sidewalks.

194

Joe Eichenbaum later said that he built a shopping center for aircraft assembly workers and their wives. He said he gave them the largest suburban department store in the country.

For a while, he was right.

Mark Taper said that owning one of his houses made the owners part of the middle class. He was wrong.

The houses never were middle class, nor were the people living in them. They became altogether something else.

195

As the planning commission hearing ended, the commissioners rolled up the bundle of engineering drawings and gave them back to Boyar. He took the heavy roll back to his office.

A few days later, road graders began stripping the recently harvested fields.

196

Louis Boyar, Mark Taper, and Ben Weingart sat with the dignitaries when the plaque honoring Clark Bonner was unveiled at the golf course.

In one newspaper photograph of the event, Clark Bonner's three grandchildren are in the foreground, unveiling the plaque that says Bonner is the founder of my city.

In another photograph, Boyar, Taper, and Weingart are standing off to one side, smiling.

197

Mrs. Taper and Mrs. Boyar attended the dinner held before the dedication of Clark Bonner's plaque. The dinner was at the golf course clubhouse.

The next day, the local newspaper described the clothes of the two women in detail. Mrs. Taper wore organdy studded with rhinestones. Mrs. Boyar wore silk taffeta. They both carried gloves.

Ben Weingart represented the three developers at the dinner. Before he spoke, the men who had known Clark Bonner talked about Bonner's vision.

County Supervisor Herbert Legg said that Weingart's suburb was not one bit different from the community Bonner had planned.

198

Mae Boyar, Louis Boyar's wife, developed arthritis when she was twenty-two. She often was in pain, even unable to walk.

She saved and borrowed the $700 Louis Boyar needed to begin a construction company when they moved to Los Angeles in 1934.

Mae Boyar died in 1960.

In 1964, ten years after Boyar's suburb incorporated as a city, the city council dedicated a new park in Mae Boyar's name.

The news story on the day after the dedication ceremony said that Boyar was in tears when he spoke.

Boyar said his wife was generous, even when they were

young and had no money. He said that she often would be so touched by the troubles of others that she could not sleep.

199

The city began buying land for the Mae Boyar Park in 1959. Part of it was purchased from a Baptist church.

The owners of the other empty lots stalled for a higher price, and most of the land had to be condemned.

Three of the property owners fought the city's appraisals until 1963.

The condemnation proceeding eventually went to trial. The city offered $145,000 for the property. A county judge required the city to pay $199,000 for the park's ten acres.

The city dedicated Mae Boyar Park on her birthday, October 3, 1964.

200

On the same day in 1957, the city dedicated three parks on land that had been set aside by the suburb's three developers.

Each park is a rectangle of playing fields next to an elementary school and surrounded by blocks of houses.

The three parks are named for Simon Bolívar, José de San Martín, and José del Valle.

Del Valle was the author of the Declaration of Independence of Central America and the president of Honduras. Bolívar's armies liberated half of South America. San Martín's armies fought the Spanish in Argentina and liberated southern Peru and Chile.

Three of my city's ten parks are named in honor of national heroes of Central and South America because of the Pan American Festival Association.

The festival association put on an annual parade in which consular officials from Central and South American countries were driven down Clark Avenue in new convertibles borrowed from car dealers.

Sometimes a former movie star was the parade's grand marshal.

Horses and riders in western outfits rode in the parade. High school bands played.

A float carried the Miss Pan American Queen and her court.

201

The festival association used to honor individual Central and South American countries in the parade. Each year, in alphabetical order, the parade recognized a different member country of the Organization of American States.

The last country honored individually was Haiti in 1978.

The following year, the association looked at the list of countries to be honored in the coming years and decided to recognize all of Latin America, not any individual country.

The association also stopped putting on a parade.

Instead, the association puts on a weekend Pan American Festival at Mayfair Park. The city helps by organizing craft and food sales and arranging for carnival rides.

Men's service clubs used to sponsor a luncheon which included a high school speech contest in both English and Spanish. The contestants spoke on the theme of pan-American friendship.

The luncheon continues, but not the speech contest.

202

Ask someone to identify Simon Bolívar, and older residents will mention South America.

Ask someone to identify José de San Martín, and usually you'll draw a blank.

In 1982, a group of Argentines from Los Angeles asked the city's permission to stage a protest against Great Britain and the Falkland Islands war. They wanted a site they thought would be symbolic. They asked to use San Martín Park.

None of us at city hall remembered the park had been named for Argentina's national hero. We forgot that the Argentine government had given the city the bronze bust of San Martín at the park's entrance.

José del Valle is less known. Even the Spanish pronunciation of his name isn't much used in the neighborhood around the park named in his honor.

The park is often called "del-val" by the college students who staff the park during the summer.

203

Newspaper reporters interviewed Taper every few years, after he stopped building houses and became a banker. The *Long Beach Press-Telegram* called him a "millionaire financier."

I interviewed Taper once, in his Beverly Hills office. I was with the city's video production crew. We were making a program celebrating the city's thirtieth anniversary of incorporation.

During the interview, Taper said that home ownership was a steadying influence on people. He believed that owning a home for the first time was enough to make a working man a good citizen.

204

I do not know what Ben Weingart believed in.

In the 1960s, when county politics and real estate development were nearly the same, newspaper reporters described Weingart as "influential."

He built the shopping center in my city, one of the most successful in the nation. He built forty-two thousand apartments, and kept them all. He kept his hotels in downtown Los Angeles, even when skid row grew up around them. He developed the Fed-Mart chain of discount stores. For several years, he was Los Angeles County's largest individual property tax payer.

In 1970, when Weingart's current business associates worried about his relationship with his former nurse, they called him "eccentric."

When they had him committed to a guarded private room at Good Samaritan Hospital in 1974, they called him "incompetent."

Weingart's business associates (who became his court-appointed conservators), Weingart's banker (who sat on the hospital board), and the doctor from Good Samaritan Hospital (who certified Weingart's incompetence) were good friends.

When he died in 1980, Weingart had holdings worth an estimated $221 million.

205

My father believed in authority. He believed that faithfulness of a particularly knowing kind could replace moral choices.

He was a good Catholic.

My father knew that the place where he lived allowed him to be a good Catholic. It allowed him to think his life might be redeemed.

Three Jews built a faithfulness into the place where I live. They built the city where my family lived and where my mother and father died.

206

When I walk to work, thinking of these stories, they seem insignificant. At Mass on Sunday, I remember them as prayers.

207

For most of us here, the extent of our concern goes no further than the surrounding tract of houses, about four hundred families.

For some residents, concern extends only to the forty-six houses on their block. That's the distance I walked once a year, when I was in grade school, to sell subscriptions to the weekly Catholic newspaper.

Seventeen percent of the city's residents have lived here twenty-five years or more. The limit of their concern is often much smaller. It embraces only the houses they see from their front porch.

They may complain about a neighbor's unkempt property or the untrimmed tree in the parkway.

The limit is tightening for the oldest residents, pulling back from the street and the sidewalk. Their landscaping grows untended, though the lawn for now is mowed by a middle-aged son or son-in-law. Their shutters are weathering where forty-five years of paint has pulled away from the wood.

Later, their concern will shrink inside the house, out of my view, where I do not follow.

208

One neighbor on my block ran a lathe. Another worked on the assembly line in a plastics plant. Another was an oil refinery worker until his death.

My father was an engineer for the Gas Company.

There was no obvious way to tell a factory worker from a business owner or a professional man when I grew up. Every house on my block looked much the same.

It's still hard to measure status. One neighbor is a cosmetics salesman. Another is a security guard at Douglas. Two more work for the city of Long Beach.

Several are now retired. Some are widows.

The man who used to live across the street owned his own painting business. He became moderately well-off repainting school buildings, and he moved away.

The family moved to Rancho Palos Verdes, a suburb with horses and swimming pools.

209

State and county grants are helping my city replace thirty-year-old playground equipment at Mae Boyar Park, as well as the three parks named for Latin American heroes.

The city's recreation department has a theme for the equipment at each park. At Bolívar Park, the preschool and school-age play equipment will have a nautical theme.

At Del Valle Park, the playground theme is transportation.

Playground equipment at San Martín Park already has a storybook theme.

There are two metal frameworks in the shape of pumpkin coaches in the park playground. These will only be repainted, because the neighborhood mothers asked that the "Cinderella coaches" not be replaced.

At Boyar Park, the theme of the playground equipment is prehistoric life.

The new equipment, which must meet the standards of the Americans with Disabilities Act, is accessible to disabled children and disabled parents.

210

According to Laura Winston, who was his nurse and then his mistress, Ben Weingart never read books. He only read the classified section of the *Los Angeles Times* to see if his rental properties were vacant.

He ate precisely the same meals every day.

He always carried several hundred dollars in half of a torn envelope.

He gave away soap and razors to the bums who hung around the skid row hotels he still owned.

He never went to the movies. Winston said he never went anywhere.

His idea of a vacation, she said, was visiting the city he had helped to build.

211

The San Gabriel River is paralleled by a trail maintained by the county for joggers and bikers. The trail goes from Long Beach to Whittier, a distance of about fifteen miles.

The trail is an asphalt path on top of the levee along the river's east bank. Several cities have developed the empty land next to the trail as a park, as my city has done.

There have been robberies on the trail. One involved a father and his infant son. The man was jogging, pushing his son in a light aluminum-and-nylon stroller.

They were confronted by three teenage boys. They demanded the man's wallet.

He was an off-duty police officer. He reached into his pack while one of the boys threatened the baby with a knife.

The man pulled out a pistol and shot the teenage boy. He was hit twice. One bullet split his spine.

Paralyzed, the boy fell backward and over the edge of the path. He slid down the sloping levee wall to the floor of the river, which is nearly always dry.

212

My mother died in 1979.

Before she died, she lived through five years of increasing disability from heart disease.

By the time she died, everything that might have been taken from her had been, even her fear.

213

Both my parents died before they were seventy, as did my mother's sister and my uncles Jack, Frank, and Ken. I am forty-six.

Given the odds, I am two-thirds through my life.

The first third I spent daydreaming. The second third, I spent waiting. The last third begins with these stories.

It is a proportion I can bear.

214

After his mother died, he chose to live here with his father. After his father died, he chose to stay here. He stayed partly because he said he would to the girl he had loved.

She is married now. She and her husband have two daughters.

They rent a house he owns. It's one of the first houses the three developers built in 1950.

He has dinner there occasionally, and makes jokes about being the landlord.

215

The grid limited our choices, exactly as urban planners said it would. But the limits weren't paralyzing.

The design of this suburb compelled a conviviality that people got used to and made into a substitute for choices, including not choosing at all.

There are an indefinite number of beginnings and endings on the grid, but you are always somewhere.

216

From 1st Street, opposite Los Angeles City Hall, numbered streets descend south across the nearly level plain formed by the Los Angeles and San Gabriel rivers.

The numbered streets as far as 33rd Street in Los Angeles are aligned with the plaza Colonel de Neve laid out in 1781. These streets are oriented at a 45-degree angle from the cardinal compass points. These streets run southeast to northwest, not east and west.

Colonel de Neve recognized a line of authority that extended back three thousand miles to the Spanish viceroy in the City of Mexico, and five thousand miles further to a book in an archive in Seville.

The book was the *Laws of the Indies.* It was a collection of royal ordinances assembled two hundred years earlier, for Philip II in 1573.

That book was based on another book on town planning, written in 25 B.C.E. by the Roman architect Vitruvius.

As he was ordered to, Colonel de Neve laid out the streets of an abstract city.

It was a city where winds blow only from the north, and where the sun each day must light the sides of a small, square house equally.

217

For about three miles—and more than a hundred years— the streets of Los Angeles preserved the bias of Colonel de Neve's drawing.

Then Los Angeles boomed as a destination for tourists and immigrants.

For a few weeks in 1887, the cost of a westbound train ticket from Chicago was only a dollar.

The newcomers remarked on the city's disturbing misalignment.

After 1901, city surveyors oriented new streets to the cardinal compass points—north, south, east, west—the way an American city is gridded.

If you look at a map of Los Angeles today, you see the intersection of the two cities. In the neighborhood streets between the freeways and the boulevards, you'll see Colonel de Neve's city in the heart of Los Angeles.

The king of Spain's city was a perfect square.

Its carefully misaligned street plan extends to the original boundaries of the city, about three miles on each side of the river.

218

School textbooks still reprint the drawing of the plaza, house lots, and rectangular fields by the river.

The textbooks show the plan of Los Angeles aligned squarely with the right angles of the page.

Sometimes the illustration includes a small, oblique arrow in the lower right corner of the map. The arrow doesn't point to the top of the page where, in the convention of map making, north is always located.

The arrow points to the upper left corner. You have to turn the book 45 degrees to see the map of Los Angeles as the king of Spain may have seen it.

219

The grid on which my city is built opens outward without limits. It's the antithesis of a ghetto.

My city will have only one gated and guarded subdivision. It's the tract of houses the real estate division of Chevron is building.

It's the only tract of houses in the city that will be shut off from the anxieties of the grid.

The new development is called Westgate. The name reminds buyers what they are getting.

220

Joseph Smith drew "The Plat of the City of Zion" in 1833. His drawing showed a city one mile square, divided by streets 132 feet wide. The streets made residential and commercial blocks of ten to fifteen acres each.

This grid could grow forever over level ground, unvarying as the number of the saints increased.

The City of Zion was built twice, in Missouri and Illinois. These Mormon towns were attacked, and their Mormon prophets lynched.

Brigham Young took the remnant of the saints into the wilderness of Utah. There, he laid out the last city of God.

221

The students at St. Timothy Lutheran School display their models of California missions in the shopping center.

The models of the missions are grouped at one end of a reflecting pool. The pools replaced the landscaped planters down the middle of the shopping mall when it was enclosed and air conditioned in 1978.

The students made their models out of cardboard, Styrofoam, plaster, and clay. Some of the models have trees made of twigs and moss.

The roofs of the models are painted red, in imitation of the red tile roofs of the original mission buildings. The walls of the models are painted pink or tan to look like stuccoed adobe.

The models are labeled with the name of the mission they represent—Santa Barbara, San Fernando, San Juan Capistrano, and San Luis Rey. The labels are a helpful concession, because all the models look much the same—a U-shape of connected one-story rooms, a two-story church partly closing the open end of the courtyard, and a low campanile for the bells.

When I was in grade school, nearly every student in the state made a model mission as part of the required California history curriculum.

Assembling one of these models, when you were eight or nine years old, made California history seem mostly about building materials.

222

William Willmore was the Los Angeles promoter for the California Immigrant Union. The backers of the Immigrant Union included the railroad trusts and the state's largest landowners.

In 1880, they encouraged Willmore to option four thousand acres of the nearly level plain at the mouth of the Los Angeles River from the Bixby family.

Willmore called the site the "American Colony."

He planned to sell house lots, as well as farms ranging in size from five to eighty acres. His "colonists" would build houses and harvest oranges and olives from orchards irrigated by their own artesian wells.

Willmore's city, except for the two hotels he planned to build, would have no saloons.

Willmore filed a subdivision map with the county in 1882. It showed a city that was eight blocks wide and ten blocks deep. The streets, where no houses stood, were oriented precisely to the cardinal points of the compass.

Willmore had the new city named after himself.

It took Willmore more than a year to recruit sixty "colonists" from Kansas farm communities. They reached Willmore City in February 1882, but few of them bought lots.

It was a rainy winter the following year, and the Methodist Resort Association declined to make Willmore City the headquarters of its annual camp meeting.

Willmore missed the first two payments on his purchase option.

223

By the end of 1884, Willmore City had only a dozen houses, and William Willmore's "colony" collapsed.

A few weeks later, developers with better financing bought the site of Willmore City.

They filed a new subdivision map with the county in 1887 that changed the name of Willmore City to Long Beach. The map kept the right-angle grid of the vacant streets in Willmore's original plan.

The developers paid Willmore $8,000 for the improvements he had made, including a water system that consisted of two shallow wells and four miles of riveted water mains.

The new developers built a $50,000, wood-frame hotel. It had the city's only saloon.

The Methodist camp meeting came to town the next summer and put a wood-frame "tabernacle" in a grove of eucalyptus trees on land the developers donated.

The developers promised there would be no more saloons.

224

As Long Beach grew, the numbered streets extended north from 1st Street to 72nd Street.

A few blocks further north is 226th Street, the last numbered street anchored in downtown Los Angeles.

The numbered streets in my city count back to Colonel de Neve's drawing of the plaza in Los Angeles.

But the house numbers count back to the center of William Willmore's map, from which his name had been removed.

225

In 1923, Long Beach annexed a worthless, hundred-foot-wide "shoestring strip" around the ten square miles of Clark family land.

Under California law, one city could not annex the unincorporated land enclosed in another city. Long Beach's narrow strip, marked on the county recorder's map in the Hall of Administration, was enough to fend off the expansion of Los Angeles.

The fiction of the "shoestring strip" did not require Long

Beach to provide municipal services to the subdivisions Clark Bonner planned to build or burden Bonner's remaining agricultural land with city taxes.

It was an arrangement Bonner and Long Beach city officials both found agreeable.

226

In 1929, Clark Bonner wanted the house numbers in his subdivision calculated from downtown Long Beach, rather than counted eastward from the plaza in Los Angeles, about fifteen miles away.

When the county engineer reviewed Bonner's plans, he saw that the empty white space on Bonner's subdivision map was bounded by a narrow black line. The line represented the hundred-foot-wide strip of the city of Long Beach that ran through the Montana Land Company's truck farms and pastures.

Because of the Long Beach annexation strip, the county engineer agreed with Bonner that the middle-class houses he planned to build should be numbered from Long Beach, not Los Angeles.

227

The line on the county recorder's map prevented Los Angeles from annexing twenty square miles of alfalfa, lima beans, hog farms, and dairies.

It also put the land that supplied Long Beach's water out of the reach of Los Angeles.

Long Beach city officials thought the line on the county

recorder's map decided the political future of the Montana Land Company's real estate developments.

They were wrong.

The Montana Land Company put up only four tracts of houses before the company was sold.

Louis Boyar, Mark Taper, and Ben Weingart put up 17,500 inexpensive houses on the land they bought from the company.

In 1953, residents of the new suburb defeated a series of annexation elections that would have brought their community into Long Beach neighborhood by neighborhood.

A year later, twelve thousand residents signed incorporation petitions. Their names were published on six pages of agate type in the local newspaper.

In March, they voted for the astonishing choice to make their still raw-looking neighborhoods a city.

228

William Willmore left Long Beach after the collapse of Willmore City. He was reported to be in Arizona. He was thought to be a victim of sunstroke.

Ten years later Willmore was found living on the Los Angeles County poor farm in Downey, about nine miles from the city that he had named after himself.

Some people set him up in a fruit and vegetable stand in Long Beach. Willmore wasn't a shopkeeper, and the business failed.

He died in January 1901, and was buried in the Long Beach city graveyard, on the southern slope of Signal Hill.

The women of the Signal Hill Civic League donated a small marker for the grave in 1913.

229

The Chamber of Commerce publishes a map of my city.

The map makes it easy to lose your way. It has no block numbers. Street names are not repeated on every block section.

The names of some streets are missing, so is the park named after Louis Boyar's wife.

If you ask, the city's planning department will make you a blueprint copy of its detailed map of the city. The map is an awkward size, two feet wide and a yard long. It's hard to fold.

The map shows every house lot in the city. The rows of lots look like the illustration of a fold of skin in a high school biology book.

230

On maps of Los Angeles County the lines of residential streets in my city branch from highways whose names and intersections have changed over time.

The boulevard that bears the name of my city was once called Cerritos Avenue. The name was changed in 1930 to help promote Clark Bonner's subdivision.

Somerset Avenue became Bellflower Boulevard. Lincoln Avenue became Candlewood Street. Los Angeles Street became Del Amo Boulevard.

Part of Studebaker Road shifted from the west side of the San Gabriel River to the east side.

Ross Avenue and Bennett Street disappeared entirely.

231

Marshall Boyar was Louis Boyar's son. He named the new streets in the subdivision his father was building.

He named Johanna Avenue for Johanna Dobkin, the daughter of his father's lawyer.

He named Flangel and Frankel streets for two former schoolmates, Harold Flangel and Jerry Frankel. Boyar said he had a hard time telling them apart in school.

He named Hackett Avenue for the comedian, Buddy Hackett. He named streets for movie actors Jean Hersholt and Gene Autry.

Streets named McKnight, Volk, McManus, and Schroll honored the men who arranged the financing for his father's company.

He named Gloria Street after an old girl friend. He named DeeBoyar after his wife.

Allred and Dollar streets were named for servicemen reported missing in action in Korea. Bomberry Street was named for Sergeant Robbie Bomberry, who survived a North Korean massacre of captured American soldiers and returned home.

He named Freckles Road after a dead cocker spaniel, run over by a car.

Boyar named streets Dwight, Eisenhower, Mamie, and Nixon.

Because Eisenhower already had streets named in his honor in cities nearby, the county engineer directed Marshall Boyar to choose different names.

Boyar was allowed to keep Nixon and Mamie.

232

Marshall Boyar considered naming streets Stevenson and Adlai. But after Eisenhower's election victory in 1952, Boyar changed his mind.

233

Robbie Bomberry's daughter, who lives in Illinois, wrote city hall with the news of her father's death.

She wanted to remind city officials that a street had been named after her father, and that he had been a hero.

234

There are eighteen people to whom the city no longer sends any mail. Mr. L is one of them.

For years, Mr. L sent back everything the city sent him. The mail was unopened, and stamped with a bewildering number of biblical and political exhortations.

Mr. L thinks the country's currency is illegal, that income taxes need not be paid, and that conspiracies of many kinds dictate the doings of government.

Mr. L doesn't like the city attorney, whose ordinances compel Mr. L to pay for weekly trash collection. Mr. L doesn't want his trash collected by the city. He says he takes it to the dump himself. He says he shouldn't have to pay for a service he doesn't use.

Under state law, the city forces Mr. L to pay his trash bill through his property tax, which Mr. L does pay, or he would lose his house.

Mr. L has a daughter.

She teaches an aerobics class for women, offered through the city's recreation department. The city offers hundreds of classes each year. The part-time instructors are paid by class registration fees.

The aerobics class is taught at a new community facility, built with state and federal park grants and named in honor of John S. Todd, the city attorney and one of the city's original incorporators.

It's a popular class.

235

I remember exactly how my father drove. He was a very good driver.

Los Angeles freeways were designed for my father's kind of driving. He was never impatient or uncontrolled. He never had an accident or received a ticket.

We drove everywhere.

236

Every family speaks its own language. The language I learned had the flavor of big cities in it.

Sometimes my mother, brother, and I ate lunch at the counter in the Woolworth's in the shopping center. Sometimes the waitress would comment on the way we spoke, and ask us if we were English.

237

I live on Graywood Avenue.

The next street west is Hazelbrook. The first street east is Faculty. These three streets, with about 140 houses, are bounded by Hedda Street and South Street.

All of my friends came from within the rectangle of these three blocks that I could reach without crossing at an intersection.

From age six to thirteen, I spent part of nearly every day and nearly all summer in the company of my brother and other boys who lived in houses like mine.

The character of those seven years is what makes a suburban childhood seem like an entire life.

238

My brother and I played Monopoly with the boy across the street and the three brothers who lived one block east.

We would begin the game on the morning of one day. It might end—after long breaks and arguments and reconciliations—two days later in someone else's house.

We made the rules up as we went along, to keep the game going as long as possible.

239

When we played Monopoly, we stretched out the game by doubling the money in the bank from other sets. We let players go into debt, ignored fines, allowed players to mortgage properties to each other, and forgave rents.

Late in the afternoon on the last day of one of these games, we would lose the point of playing. We moved the metal tokens around the board and realized that no one could win under these rules.

By consent, the game ended when the first player was finally called to dinner.

240

Chevron's real estate division decided to auction off the street names in its new subdivision as a fund raiser for the YMCA.

Several city council members bid successfully for a street name of their own. One city official paid to have a street named after his daughter.

I paid $200 to have a street named after my family.

The street is a cul-de-sac at the border of the city. There are eighteen houses on the dead-end street. The houses there are more than double the size of mine.

Behind them, beyond a high cinder-block wall, is a trailer park built on a landfill in the city of Long Beach.

241

As a boy, I made cities in the dirt behind my house.

After school, and on summer afternoons, Billy C and I knelt on the grass at the edge of my mother's garden, under the window to the room I shared with my brother.

We played where my mother's enormous rose bushes hung over our heads.

We laid out roads, parking lots, and rows of roofless houses with pale dirt walls. Sometimes Billy and I uncovered a bone or half of the smooth white jaw of a cat buried beneath the roses.

242

Billy C and I made garages for the metal trucks my mother bought at the big Woolworth's store in the shopping center.

The rows of dirt garage walls, as high as the width of a boy's palm, would harden in the two or three hours we played.

Some of the trucks were cast from dies made before the war. The trucks preserved the aerodynamic designs of the 1930s. They were painted in primary colors—blue, yellow, and red.

Sometimes we left a truck in the dirt, and it would disappear before we returned another day to dig.

The lost trucks turned up, sometimes years later, in the garden. They had nearly no paint. Their wire axles were rusted, and the rubber tires were gone.

243

The dirt in my backyard is part sand and part clay. It's part of the Chino soil series.

In 1917, the Bureau of Soils of the Department of Agriculture classified most of the soil now covered by houses and lawns as Chino clay loam.

This soil had been carried away from the San Gabriel Mountains only ten thousand years ago.

As late as 1914, the runoff from foothill canyons was allowed to flow unchecked into the vague rivers of the coastal plain. They dropped new sand and clay over soil deposited by older rivers during the late Pleistocene.

The rivers of the coastal plain found new beds almost every winter. Every summer, the rivers disappeared.

Where the ground dipped slightly, as it does here, the rivers concentrated alkali. It made mediocre land for wheat or barley, but it was good enough for growing sugar beets.

When sugar beet production declined in the 1920s, the truck farmers who leased the land from the Montana Land Company alternated crops of carrots, lima beans, and alfalfa.

Most of the farmers, before 1942, were Japanese.

244

My mother came to Southern California in 1943, while my father was serving as gunnery officer on the destroyer *Bradford*. The *Bradford*'s home port was Long Beach. My mother worked there as an escrow clerk in a bank.

The *Bradford*'s duty throughout the war in the Pacific was to serve as an escort ship for carrier operations. The *Bradford* directed fighter aircraft, monitored radar, and screened carriers from Japanese submarines and torpedo planes.

The *Bradford* also collected downed Navy flyers whose planes were too damaged or low on fuel to reach the carriers from which they were launched.

The crew members of the *Bradford* never lost a pilot they were sent to find.

In two years of bitter fighting, no sailor on board was killed in enemy action. In the battles for Iwo Jima and Okinawa, where kamikaze aircraft sank or damaged more than thirty ships, the *Bradford* was unharmed.

The war ended, and my parents stayed in Southern California.

They stayed a continent away from my father's mother in New York City.

They bought a house on a street that ended, for a few years, in bean fields.

245

Don Rochlen, the publicist who promoted the new suburb, told reporters from Los Angeles newspapers that the house lots in the new suburb were made small by design so that the streets could be wider.

The houses are close enough so that you might hear, if you listened, a neighbor's baby cry, a father arguing with a teenage son, or a television playing early on a summer night.

Most things here are close enough for comfort.

246

Once, my father and I watched a rerun of *Victory at Sea* in the small middle bedroom where my parents kept the television set.

It was early evening, and my father had just come home from work at the Gas Company offices in Los Angeles.

He sat next to me on the bed. I was ten or eleven years old.

I already knew my father had been in the Navy in the war, because I had seen his officer's uniform in a suitcase in the attic.

The episode of *Victory at Sea* was about the invasion of

Okinawa. We looked at the black-and-white images of ships in formation before the battle. He said we might see the *Bradford*, the ship he had been on.

We saw Japanese fighters and torpedo planes attack the ships. We saw the air around the ships fill with the small, black-and-white explosions of antiaircraft shells. We saw kamikaze planes burst into flames—in the air, as some struck the water, and when one hit an American ship.

We didn't see the *Bradford*.

247

My city doesn't have a cemetery. Louis Boyar didn't include one in his plan.

It won't ever have one. There's not enough empty space left to lay a cemetery out.

Most of the Catholic dead of my city lie in All Souls Cemetery. The cemetery is in Long Beach, on the other side of the railroad line that William A. Clark bought.

The Catholic cemetery isn't very big. It's a rectangle of land between a neighborhood shopping center and a former milk processing plant.

The cemetery grounds are level. There are no monuments on the expanse of lawn. There aren't many trees.

The layout of the cemetery's streets is a simple grid of connected ovals.

A hundred feet beyond the last row of graves at All Souls Cemetery, across the railroad tracks to the east, are the backyards of houses in my city.

The row of house roofs makes a dark, irregular pattern, punctuated by the crowns of mature trees.

It once was traditional in Christian burials that the dead lie east to west in their graves. The dead faced east. It is from the east, from Jerusalem, that Christ is expected to come to raise the dead.

Not all the graves in All Souls Cemetery are oriented this way. The graves of my parents, by chance, face east, toward the city in which I live.

248

In 1951, Emmett Gossett suffocated when a mound of sand collapsed on him. Gossett was nine years old.

He had gone with a friend to play near the equipment that pulverized river gravel into the sand used for the stucco walls of the new houses the three developers were putting up.

The boys began playing at the base of a hopper, where a partial load of sand had been taken away. The remaining sand, slightly damp, formed a wall higher than a grown man.

Gossett dug into its base and the wall of unstable sand collapsed. The efforts of the other boy to free Gossett caused even more sand to cover him.

Workmen at the cement plant, and county fire fighters when they arrived, failed to resuscitate the boy.

He was buried at All Souls Cemetery.

249

The cities Billy C and I built in my mother's garden all ended in the same way.

We took my father's garden hose and laid it some feet

away from the rows of houses and garages. One of us turned the water on so that it barely flowed.

In a few minutes, the water would pool at one end of the main street in our dirt city. A little later, water would pour through the doorways and fill up the rooms. The mud walls melted.

250

My city is concerned about disaster.

County and state agencies evaluated their response to the Northridge earthquake and warned city officials that communities like mine will be on their own for three days following a major earthquake.

Police and fire departments will be overwhelmed. The Red Cross and National Guard will concentrate in urban areas, not in these neighborhoods of small houses.

In preparation, the city is trying to get residents to change their habits.

I've written articles for the Chamber of Commerce newspaper urging residents to keep a three-day supply of food and water at home and to carry clothing and simple camping equipment in their car.

I've taped educational programs on earthquake preparedness for the city's cable channel.

I once interviewed Dr. Kate Hutton, a seismologist at the California Institute of Technology, about the risks of being in one of these stucco and chicken-wire houses during a major earthquake.

Dr. Hutton talked about houses sliding off their foundations and the dangers of flying glass and falling bookshelves.

Apart from that, she said, these houses were about the safest place you could be.

251

These postwar houses were built so lightly that they might even shelter us in a major earthquake.

The burden of our habits may do the same.

I avoided most of my father's Catholicism, but I still live here.

252

Sometimes I think the only real forces here are circumstance and grace.

.

253

The danger here during a major earthquake is liquefaction.

In a wet year, the water table is only three or four feet from the ground's surface in some parts of the city where I live. Prolonged shaking during an earthquake causes the loose, alluvial soil to shift, letting the water wick upward.

In less than a minute, solid ground flows under the weight of the structures built on it.

Tall buildings sink. Horizontal buildings crack and fall apart. Square, frame houses may slide off their foundations.

In the 1960s, California disaster planners recognized this and mapped the region's liquefaction zones.

On the maps of my city, the areas of potential liquefaction are the beds of buried rivers.

254

Fifty feet beneath my house is the Bellflower aquiclude, a thick layer of clay that traps the Artesia aquifer under it. The Artesia aquifer is a fifty-foot-thick layer of sand and gravel that was once a river bed.

It still is, in a way.

The Artesia aquifer flows with water that fell as rain and snow forty miles away and thirty years ago in the San Gabriel Mountains.

At 225 feet is the Gage aquifer, the bed of another river that drained a younger range of mountains. At 300 feet is the San Pedro Formation, another layer of impermeable clay and silt.

At 350 feet is the Hollydale aquifer. At 500 feet is the Jefferson aquifer.

These aquifers were once rivers that flowed across the Los Angeles plain into a shallow bay of the Pacific Ocean.

Beneath Jefferson aquifer, the Lynwood aquifer traces a slope that begins at 400 feet and descends below 600 feet. The Silverado aquifer begins at 450 feet and drops below 1,000 feet. The Sunnyside aquifer appears at 900 feet and disappears below 1,100 feet.

The layers of sand, gravel, and isolating clay are at least 11,000 feet thick.

Beneath them, two miles below my house, is a wide, nameless valley.

255

In 1947, the California Department of Natural Resources reported that the pattern of wet and dry years on the Los Angeles plain could be mapped back to 1385.

The record is in the tree rings of big-cone spruce trees in the San Gabriel Mountains.

The longest drought, recorded in the grain of the wood, was 43 years.

More recent tree ring data suggest that rainfall has been unusually high for the past 150 years, despite 24 years of drought between 1910 and 1934.

Geologists give the classification "semiarid" to a terrain where rainfall is between 10 and 20 inches a year. In the 127 years between 1877 and 1994, the average rainfall here was 14.9 inches.

By this definition, the Los Angeles plain is semiarid.

It's not exactly a desert.

256

The aquifers that reach the western edge of the Los Angeles plain are cut through by blocks of older rock lifted up by the collision of the Pacific Plate with the American continent.

These rocks bulge and fold underground. The folding is called an anticline.

In some places, the anticline across the western margin of the plain is revealed by a line of low hills.

This diagonal line is the Newport-Inglewood fault, which caused the 1933 Long Beach earthquake.

The anticline acts like a dam. Ground water, under pressure from the flow higher on the underground slope, collects where the rock intruded into the layers of sand and clay.

Manuel Nieto built his square, adobe house where the intruding rocks brought a shallow aquifer to the surface to form an artesian spring.

In 1881, William Willmore promised water flowing from his artesian wells to irrigate the olive and walnut trees the "colonists" of Willmore City never planted.

In 1895, a real estate promoter named Edward Bouton tapped the artesian zone north of the anticline and brought in a well that produced more than three million gallons of water a day.

257

General Edward Bouton had been a Civil War hero. When the war began, he sold a successful grain business in Chicago and raised a volunteer company of artillery at his own expense.

When the war ended he came to Los Angeles, bought the San Jacinto Rancho, and raised sheep.

He later became a real estate speculator.

With the founding of Willmore's American Colony, Bouton began to speculate in water.

He bought a section of land north of Willmore City where the low hills showed that the underlying rock had been forced upward.

Signal Hill and the Dominguez Hills mark the southwest margin of the "artesian belt" between the Los Angeles and San Gabriel rivers.

Bouton's land included a wet season marsh. It had once been a bed of the Los Angeles River.

Bouton knew the residents of Long Beach, about five miles away, needed a reliable source of water. He knew the new city's wells went down only eighty feet. The wells ran nearly dry in summer.

The Long Beach wells were on the wrong side of the underground barrier between the "artesian belt" and the ocean.

Bouton's property was on the right side.

258

General Bouton brought in his first producing well at 339 feet. He immediately sold stock in a new water company.

Most of the company's stock was bought by the owners of the Terminal Railroad.

Bouton began another well, a few dozen feet away.

When the second well came in at 750 feet, the force of the water ripped the two-inch-thick iron cap from the wellhead. Cobblestones and gravel rocketed out of the twelve-inch casing.

For days, the jet of water stood eighty feet above the well mouth.

The well shot four million gallons of water a day into the air, turning the well site into a temporary lake.

Special rail excursions from Los Angeles brought gawkers to watch the water gushing from Bouton's well.

Local papers said the column of water, shining with the afternoon sun behind it, could be seen from as far away as Whittier, ten miles north.

259

The water from General Bouton's well was slightly yellow and tasted of hydrogen sulfide.

Bouton said the yellow color came from the buried peat beds through which the water flowed. The peat made the water naturally soft.

He also said the water was well known in Los Angeles as a cure for kidney and rheumatic diseases.

He said that Professor E. W. Hilgard and Professor R. H. Loughbridge, chemists from the state university at Berkeley, had examined the water.

They would testify to its healthful properties.

260

The Bouton Well, when it was finally capped, supplied all of Long Beach's water for nearly ten years.

Bouton's company marketed the water with the slogan, "It does not see the light of day until it flashes and sparkles from the faucet in your home."

The water came in such abundance and with so little effort that people in Long Beach thought there was a lake of pure, fresh water in a cavern under the city.

261

Water company employees laid redwood pipes to bring water from the Bouton Well to Long Beach.

The milled and hollow redwood logs, bound with iron

straps, had a bore of twenty-four inches. That was big enough for a man to crawl through.

The redwood pipes lasted two generations, serving even the first years of my city's development, until the wood soaked through completely and the tree-trunk pipes sagged shut.

In the early 1950s, when the wooden lines were taken out of service, the limp sections were grubbed out of the ground by a future employee of my city, working in the sun on the metal seat of a backhoe.

262

In 1900, five years after General Bouton began supplying all of Long Beach's water, William A. Clark bought the Terminal Railroad, its franchise to build a transcontinental rail connection to Utah, and control of Bouton's water company.

He had already bought ten square miles of pasture from the Bixby family, owners of what remained of Manuel Nieto's hundreds of empty square miles. The land lay across nearly the entire width of the "artesian belt" between the San Gabriel and Los Angeles rivers.

Clark sold the railroad to the Union Pacific. He sold Bouton's water company to Long Beach.

263

In 1903, the Bouton Well was still flowing at the rate of nearly three million gallons of water a day. But the lake created by the Bouton Well had dried up.

Then the level of the well dropped, and the water

stopped flowing. The water company installed electric pumps to bring the water to the surface.

1914 was one of the wettest years on record. The Los Angeles, San Gabriel, and Santa Ana rivers flooded. Water stood five feet deep in some parts of William A. Clark's beet fields.

The flow from the Bouton Well was sporadic. It produced water just five months that winter, and only three months in the winter of 1915.

A nineteen-year drought began.

There had been 107,000 acres of Los Angeles plain in the "artesian belt." By 1919, artesian wells flowed on only 32,000 acres.

In 1919, the mayor of Long Beach said the supply of water from the city's twenty wells was inexhaustible.

By 1933, there was no "artesian belt" at all and most wells drew from aquifers that were below sea level.

By then, the city of Long Beach had abandoned the Bouton Well.

264

Clark Bonner began development of the Clark family's land in 1929 by selling Long Beach a thin, shotgun-shaped section of former beet fields.

The strip of land stretched from the San Gabriel River to the edge of the subdivision Bonner planned to build. It ran through fields the Montana Land Company still leased to tenant farmers every year.

The land was more valuable for the right to take water from it than to build houses on it or to grow any crop, even if wells were near the practical limit for production.

Long Beach needed more water until the Colorado River Aqueduct could be completed, and that was at least a decade away.

By law in California, if you own the land you own the right to take anything you can from it. It's a miner's law.

Cities and real estate promoters were already pumping billions of gallons of water a year from the aquifers under the Los Angeles plain. As they drilled down through the layers of gravel and clay, they named them for the subdivisions that lay over them.

Sunnyside, the deepest aquifer, has the same name as a cemetery.

Early in 1930, Long Beach water department workers began drilling beneath the strip of fields the city had bought from the Montana Land Company. The workmen bore into water-bearing sand in the Silverado aquifer at 1,700 feet.

The water came up hot.

It was ninety-three degrees.

265

By the mid-1930s, Long Beach had expanded the "shotgun strip" into a ribbon of land 660 feet wide and 6 miles long across the entire southeastern edge of the former "artesian belt."

The city bought the land to extract as much water from it as it could.

Nearly all the water-bearing land was outside Long Beach city limits.

Originally, state law had limited ground water extraction

to the immediate use of the land owner, but state courts now allowed property owners to pipe water from their wells anywhere they wished.

Colonel Charles Heartwell, the chairman of the Long Beach Water Commission, advocated sinking as many wells as possible along the length of the city's six-mile strip.

When some of the Montana Land Company's "shotgun strip" was turned into a park, grateful Long Beach city officials named it after Colonel Heartwell.

266

The Montana Land Company got the abandoned Bouton Well as part of the sale of the "shotgun strip" to Long Beach.

Part of the well site was an irrigation pond in a trough where Bouton Lake had been. The land around the pond was too wet for building, but Clark Bonner thought it could be made into a golf course.

In 1934, Bonner hired William Bell, a well-known course designer, to lay a golf course out.

Bell had Bonner's workmen dig a twenty-acre lake as a water hazard and for irrigation storage. The workmen lined the five-foot-deep lake bed with clay to hold irrigation water for the greens and fairways of the golf course.

Bonner named his lake after the one created by the spectacular Bouton Well in 1895. The two artificial Bouton lakes were roughly in the same location.

The golf course water hazard is still listed as Bouton Lake on county maps.

Today, the southern end is separated from the rest of Bouton Lake by a concrete barrier. Under an agreement with the county, Long Beach uses this end of the lake to store reclaimed water.

During the day, electric pumps fill this part of the lake with processed effluent from Long Beach's water reclamation plant.

At night, the reclaimed water is pumped away and sprayed over playing fields and park lawns in Long Beach.

267

Between 1910 and 1950, water companies, cities, and land developers extracted as much cheap water as they could from the layers of aquifers under the Los Angeles plain.

Extracting water from an aquifer is called drafting. When more water is taken than runoff replaces, the aquifer is said to be overdrafted.

By 1930, the rate of overdrafting on the Los Angeles plain was 24 percent, and the rate was increasing each year.

To find any water at all, new wells had to go below 750 feet. Some went below 1,500 feet.

Hundreds of shallow wells in the cities around Long Beach went dry.

The overdrafting caused subsidence. After pumpers extracted the water, the formerly saturated layers of sand and gravel sagged. Whole neighborhoods began to sink one or two feet.

Overdrafting the aquifers caused a more serious problem.

Test wells in the 1940s in Long Beach began to bring up brine.

268

When Louis Boyar, Mark Taper, and Ben Weingart bought the Montana Land Company, they acquired the right to take all the water they could from under the company's land.

The three developers immediately made plans to sell the water to the owners of the 17,500 houses they were going to build.

They drilled new wells, laid a network of four-inch water mains, and installed a meter and service line for each house.

They put up steel storage tanks where the Montana Land Company had located its field headquarters, in a stand of eucalyptus trees on Arbor Road.

By 1957, seven years later, there wasn't any profit in running their water company.

Boyar, Taper, and Weingart sold it to my city. The city paid for the water company by issuing $5 million in revenue bonds at 4.1 percent interest.

The real asset was not the company's wells, mains, and service lines. These would have to be replaced eventually and, as the city administrator pointed out to the city council, the company's water mains were undersize anyway.

The item of real value was the right to take the water.

269

The anticline along the Newport-Inglewood fault is enough to slow the movement of water through the layers of aquifers, but it isn't a perfect barrier.

Some of the aquifers extend over the anticline. Other aquifers pass around it, where the Los Angeles and San Gabriel rivers reach Long Beach.

This water is important, but not for drinking.

It holds back the sea.

270

Most of the Los Angeles plain is less than 300 feet above sea level. The aquifers are as much as a quarter-mile below it.

In the 1940s, industrial pumping on the western edge of the plain overdrafted some of the aquifers. The over-drafting caused a localized drop in the pressure of the underground water.

Without the pressure of the water, the Pacific Ocean began to reclaim some of its buried estuaries.

Today, there is a saline plume under the city of Torrance. It's fifty-seven billion gallons of undrinkable water.

This salt water is moving. It's still sinking into the basin and traveling toward Los Angeles at the rate of 300 to 400 feet a year.

A line of observation wells tracks its progress under the plain.

The fresh water flowing west toward the Newport-Inglewood fault is pumped to the surface and delivered to the faucets of 1.2 million households, including those in my city.

The salt water is on the other side of the fault.

Intrusion of the saline plume past the fault line would be a disaster for forty-three cities.

It would make drought on the Los Angeles plain permanent.

271

Mayfair Pool was open all summer when I was growing up. No one in my neighborhood could afford a big backyard swimming pool.

There were so many school-age children that a single two-block area might have more than 150.

On hot afternoons, you would walk to the pool with your trunks on under your jeans and carry a towel. You would wait in the heat in a long line of other children, change in the crowded locker room, and quickly step onto the pool deck.

The shallow end of the pool would be so full of younger children that you could not swim. Many of the children would be pressed along the edge of the pool, holding on to the coping of the concrete deck.

The crowd would gradually shift some children into the less-crowded, deep end of the pool.

If you could swim, or were brave, you got away from the pool edge and struck out across the deep water.

272

The city of Los Angeles has just enough water for its needs. Most of this water is piped from the Owens Valley. Long Beach has just enough water delivered from state and federal water projects, and from its own wells.

My city, and forty-two others, have just enough water drawn from the aquifers beneath their neighborhoods.

We have just enough because cities and land owners with

water rights finally agreed to hold off the disaster of saltwater intrusion into the basin's freshwater aquifers.

They turned to the county courts in 1959 for adjudication of their pumping rights and a limit on how much water they can take each year.

The court appointed a San Gabriel River watermaster to oversee the ebbing of the ground water.

The watermaster accounts for the extraction of every gallon of water under a plan the pumpers have voluntarily agreed to follow.

Another independent agency, the Southern California Water Replenishment District, is responsible for preventing the Pacific Ocean from reclaiming its former bay.

Every gallon taken from the aquifers under the plain is supposed to be replaced, to maintain the precarious balance of salt water and fresh water.

The replenishment district oversees a system of check dams and spreading grounds. In a year of normal rain, this system holds about 24 billion gallons of runoff long enough for it to sink into the sand and gravel of the current bed of the San Gabriel River.

273

That isn't enough to recharge the aquifers.

Every year, the replenishment district blends 17 billion gallons of reclaimed waste water with fresh water from the Colorado River and pumps the mixture onto the San Gabriel River spreading grounds.

The reclaimed water disappears into the ground along with the winter's runoff.

This isn't enough to maintain hydrostatic pressure in the saltwater intrusion zones.

Electric pumps force fresh water through perforated steel casings driven into the depleted aquifers.

Think of the pumps as reverse wells.

The replenishment district maintains four barriers to saltwater intrusion. The barriers are made of twelve billion gallons of fresh water pumped back into the aquifers each year. Two of the freshwater barriers are at the borders of my city.

A third barrier slows the plume under Torrance.

By an accident of geology, my city's sixteen wells pump from aquifers maintained by the replenishment district's injection program.

Much of the water that my city delivers to residents originally came from the California Aqueduct and the Colorado River, from hundreds of miles away.

274

My city acquired the right to the water under its neighborhoods when the city bought the water company Louis Boyar, Mark Taper, and Ben Weingart had formed.

The three developers bought the right to the water from The Montana Land Company.

The company got its rights from the Bixby family, who bought them with the land from Don Juan Temple, who married into them through his wife Rafaela Cota, who received them as an inheritance from her grandfather Manuel Nieto, who was provisionally granted them by the governor of California, who had them by right of possession of the king of Spain.

Most people who live on the semiarid Los Angeles plain cannot explain precisely where their water comes from.

The rivers, spreading grounds, dams, injection wells, and aqueducts are part of a landscape people rarely notice.

275

When it rains hard here, flood control channels fill quickly. In a few minutes the water can rise higher than your head, and it flows faster than you can run.

I grew up when my neighborhood was crossed by unfenced flood control channels, where boys in packs of four or five played after school and on weekends.

Hunting for frogs in the rain in one of the channels, boys would sometimes be caught in the suddenly rising water. Neighborhood parents, or the fire department, rescued them when they could. Once a boy drowned in one of the channels; another boy drowned in a flooded sump.

Frightened and angry parents petitioned the County Board of Supervisors to improve the ditches. The county built cement walls and chain-link fences.

When the channels were cemented and fenced, the frogs disappeared from them, along with the boys.

276

When it rains lightly and steadily, the replenishment district's system of dams and spreading grounds collects the runoff from the San Gabriel River. On parts of the Los

Angeles River, the runoff gathers behind rubber dams, inflated only when it rains.

When it rains harder, the dams and gravel basins designed to capture runoff become part of a flood control system intended to move the water as quickly as possible.

Along most city streets, storm drains open into feeder channels that empty directly into the rivers.

When it rains very hard—an inch of rain an hour—the Los Angeles and San Gabriel rivers quickly fill nearly to the top of the concrete levees the Army Corps of Engineers built to contain flood water.

The Corps of Engineers built the levees, beginning in 1938, to prevent the two rivers from cutting new channels through nearly 300 square miles of suburban development.

When the two rivers flow at capacity, millions of gallons of flood water move through them in just a few hours.

To prevent the flood water from topping the levees, the Corps designed flap gates that close the feeder channels until the crest passes.

When the flap gates close, the excess water has to be stored somewhere. The flood control system stores the water on the level streets of the cities on the Los Angeles plain.

277

Until the Corps of Engineers built the county's flood control system, the Los Angeles and San Gabriel were called "tramp" rivers because they found a new bed almost every winter.

In the 1880s, the bed of the San Gabriel River would routinely shift more than a mile west after a heavy rain.

The Los Angeles River once entered the Pacific Ocean near the city of Santa Monica and then at San Pedro, eighteen miles away. Once, the Los Angeles River was completely captured by the San Gabriel River.

In 1915, levees began to limit the wandering of the two rivers, although they sometimes overflowed their new, artificial banks. A series of disastrous floods in the 1930s led to the construction of the concrete flood control channels.

The concrete channels move water faster. They also make flooding more predictable.

My city is between the two rivers.

Some of their former beds are hidden in the city's landscape, until it rains hard enough.

When it does, the flap gates of the feeder channels close. Water gathers in gutters and sometimes spreads over the flat streets. A few intersections become impossible to cross.

Water may top the curb in some places and spread over the parkway strip between the street and sidewalk.

278

When the city was built, bulldozers piled the soil left over from grading the streets onto the house lots.

The bulldozers moved four million cubic yards of soil.

In most neighborhoods, the house lots were raised two or three feet higher than the roadway surface.

I do not know if the three developers saw the raised lots as a solution to the problem of building houses in what is, geologically, a river bed.

Disposing of the leftover dirt, however, would have been very expensive.

279

The damage caused by deliberately storing flood water on city streets is not extensive.

Understandably, the city gets complaints from drivers whose cars stall in flooded intersections, and from the residents of neighborhoods where water is standing in driveways.

When they call city hall, I explain that the system protects them from catastrophe by flooding their streets from time to time.

280

I tell my tenants' oldest daughter stories about my brother and my parents.

I tell her about my brother's first electric train set and the mysterious light it made as the train circled in our room on Christmas morning.

I tell her about the week in 1953 when it rained with no letup and all the streets flooded.

I tell her about the time my brother, not yet four, took all the knobs off the doors in our house. He used a kitchen spoon to take out the screws.

I tell her about the time my brother jimmied open the aluminum window screen in his room, jumped out, and wandered away wearing only a diaper. He was two then.

Sheriff's deputies found him walking on Clark Avenue in Bellflower, about a mile away.

I tell her what my father said, and what my mother did.

My tenants' oldest daughter is five. She wants to hear all the stories I have.

281

It is unlawful to tell the future in my city. One of the oldest ordinances in the city code book, adopted when the city incorporated in 1954, lists the illegal practices by which the future may not be foretold.

It is illegal to furnish any information "not otherwise obtainable by the ordinary processes of knowledge by means of any occult psychic power, faculty or force, clairvoyance, clairaudience, cartomancy, psychology, psychometry, phrenology, spirits, seership, prophecy, augury, astrology, palmistry, necromancy, mind-reading, telepathy, or by any other craft, art, science, talisman, charm, potion, magnetism, magnetized substance, gypsy cunning or foresight, crystal gazing, or oriental mysteries."

282

According to the 1990 Census, my city has a population of 73,557. It had a population of more than 83,000 in 1970.

As the city's residents aged, the size of each household got smaller. Older children grew up and moved away.

New families moving in had fewer children.

The Census reports that 72 percent of the residents are white, 15 percent are Hispanic, 4 percent are African American, and 3 percent are Filipino.

283

In 1940, the Douglas Aircraft Company began building a new assembly plant at the edge of the Long Beach Airport. It was across the street from the "semi-sustaining" house lots Charles Hopper was still trying to sell.

At the request of the Army, Clark Bonner had sold Donald Douglas the land for the aircraft plant the year before.

The Douglas workers assembling B-17 bombers for the War Department needed places to live.

Bonner turned over 650 acres of lima bean fields to John Griffith and Herbert Legg. Their real estate company subdivided some of the acreage into fifty-by-one-hundred-foot lots.

Shortly after the Douglas plant opened in 1941, the company distributed a sales brochure for the new houses it was putting up.

One side of the brochure is a map. It shows the subdivision's convenient location, on a main highway between Los Angeles and Long Beach.

The guide describes the country club and tells potential buyers that it's open to all residents of the new subdivision.

The other side of the brochure is a list of "one hundred reasons why you should live here."

Reason eleven is "churches of all denominations." Number seventeen is "Good Humor Man." Number twenty-two is "telephones." Number forty-nine is "good radio reception."

Number sixty is "healthy soil." Sixty-one is "deep rock well water."

284

The sales brochure lists the last of the reasons to live here under the heading "100% American Family Community."

These reasons are arranged as answers to a series of questions.

The first question is "race restrictions?" The answer is yes.

The second question is "residential restrictions?" The answer is yes.

The fourteenth question is "carefully planned home on each lot?" The answer is yes.

The eighteenth question asks if the new subdivision is the "white spot" of Long Beach.

The answer is yes.

285

Herbert Legg left the real estate development company and ran for office.

He became a county supervisor.

286

In 1940, Long Beach had 164,271 residents. It had a black population of 2,000.

Jobs at defense plants, desegregated by presidential order during the war, brought the number of black Residents to 15,000 in 1950.

By 1960, the number had dwindled to 9,500.

In 1947, city officials in Long Beach had demolished part of the federal housing built for war workers. The city tore down the part segregated for Negroes and left standing the part reserved for whites.

That had eliminated 190 families.

Real estate agents steered black families away from Mayfair and the newer subdivisions to neighborhoods in Compton and Willowbrook.

The war-surplus beacon on the steel derrick that identified the suburb Boyar, Taper, and Weingart were building attracted tens of thousands of potential buyers every week.

If they were black, they didn't stay long.

The Federal Housing Authority made it possible to build the houses and offer them to men who sometimes made less than a hundred dollars a week.

Still, the sales staff refused to accept applications from Negro families.

In 1960, six years after residents of my suburb voted for incorporation, the city was still 98.5 percent white.

The Census that year counted seven people—in a population of 67,125—who admitted they were black.

287

In 1953, the Levittown on Long Island had a population of nearly 70,000. It was the largest community in the nation with no Negroes at all.

288

When I was a boy, about a third of my neighbors came from the border South.

That meant that they, or their parents, had come to California from Oklahoma, Texas, Missouri, Arkansas, or Kansas.

Some were the children of real Dust Bowl Okies.

In the mid-1930s, their fathers had worked as migrant farm laborers in the San Joaquin Valley. The fathers of luckier ones had occasional jobs in the Kern County oil fields.

Those who had come to Los Angeles tried to find work as mechanics' helpers or in construction. It often took a month or more to find any sort of job, even picking oranges or working in a packing shed for three dollars a day.

It took a year to establish California residency and qualify for public assistance.

If a family's money ran out, as it often did, state agencies offered assistance only if the family agreed to leave California and return home.

Very few families accepted.

If a man could string out a year of intermittent jobs, he would be eligible for a state relief check or a federal job from the Works Progress Administration.

If he got a WPA job, he could plant trees or pour concrete for new sidewalks.

289

When the war began, the Okies were ready for work.

Ten percent of wartime federal spending went to California. Southern California aircraft plants produced 40 percent of the planes flown by the Navy and Army Air Corps.

In 1942, between 30 and 50 percent of new employees at Southern California aircraft plants came originally from the states of the border South.

At the Douglas plant in Long Beach, 87 percent of them were women. They made sixty cents an hour.

By the end of the war, 600,000 border Southerners had migrated to Southern California to work in defense industries.

Ernie Pyle called them Aviation Okies.

Pyle said the new migrants were already filling the cities of Torrance and El Monte, as well as Bell Gardens, one of several low-cost, blue-collar communities between the Los Angeles and San Gabriel rivers.

By 1950, the Aviation Okies began buying houses in my suburb with the money they had saved working at Douglas Aircraft, North American Aviation, or the Long Beach Naval Shipyard.

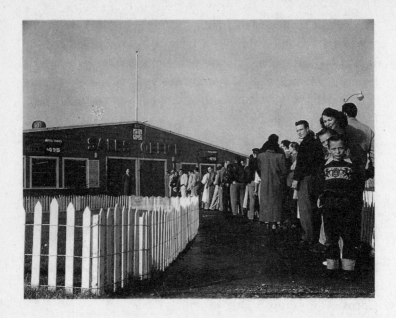

290

It wasn't easy for some young couples to come up with the $695 down payment.

They might have to wait a year to save that much from a young man's salary.

291

In 1954, a few months after my suburb had incorporated as a city, Louis Boyar and Ben Weingart were subpoenaed to testify before a Senate subcommittee.

The subcommittee asked more than a dozen developers

to explain irregularities in their federally backed mortgages and construction loans.

Senator Homer Capehart of Indiana, the chairman of the subcommittee, was bewildered by Weingart's answers.

Weingart explained that he was a director of 200 to 300 development companies and he couldn't be expected to remember how each one operated.

Senator Capehart said "We seem to know more about your companies than you do yourself."

Weingart smiled and said, "You probably do, but you don't have as many companies as I do."

When Senator Capehart asked if most of these were dummy corporations, Weingart said, "You'll have to ask Mr. Boyar."

Weingart answered so many questions with "ask Mr. Boyar" that Senator Capehart wondered aloud how Weingart, with investments worth $200 million, could know so little about his own business.

Weingart said, "That's why I have Mr. Boyar."

292

Senator Capehart accused Weingart of setting up 200 or 300 dummy corporations merely to shield his investments.

If any one of Weingart's companies failed, the FHA loan it controlled would default to the federal government. Weingart had nothing to lose.

Senator Capehart asked if that was true.

Weingart said, "You'll have to ask Mr. Boyar."

293

Louis Boyar and Ben Weingart financed the building of most of the houses in my city using an obscure section of the National Housing Act.

Under Section 213, the FHA would provide 100-percent financing for construction, but only if the houses were built by a nonprofit cooperative of property owners.

The amount of land one of these cooperatives could develop and the size of its FHA loan were limited by law. The maximum number of houses that could be built under section 213 was 501.

Section 213 was a New Deal program. It assisted rural communities by encouraging property owners to organize a nonprofit building association to put up affordable housing.

Boyar and Weingart used Section 213 to finance the largest suburban development in the nation.

There was nothing illegal about it.

294

Just before Thanksgiving in 1952, the regional director of the FHA held a brief ceremony in the middle of a street of recently built houses.

The ceremony celebrated the completion of another 3,125 housing units in the suburb the three developers were building.

The FHA regional director explained how restrictions on lending had ended no-down-payment mortgages at the start of the Korean War. The restrictions had stopped construction of the new suburb until FHA mortgage guarantees were arranged under Section 213.

He reminded the audience that 75 percent of the home-owners in the project were buying a house for the first time.

Louis Boyar and Mark Taper spoke. They expressed their appreciation to federal and county officials for their assistance.

County Supervisor Herbert Legg also spoke, as did the city manager of Long Beach, the president of the Chamber of Commerce, and the publisher of the Long Beach newspaper.

Don Rochlen was the master of ceremonies.

He told the audience that the new suburb now had seven elementary schools with four more under construction.

He told them the average family head in the new suburb was thirty-two years old and that he made $4,313 a year.

295

Boyar, Taper, and Weingart controlled the cooperatives fronted by their employees, who applied for financing under Section 213.

A few of the employees lived in the houses the three men were putting up. Most didn't.

The dummy cooperatives bought land from the developers' real estate company, making a profit for the developers of $1,600 an acre.

The nonprofit associations then contracted with another corporation controlled by the three developers to put up the houses.

Prospective buyers picked a floor plan and a lot at the developers' sales office. Nonveterans made a down payment, depending on the size of the house, of either $695 or $795.

Veterans paid a token $195 down.

The down payment was actually the purchase of stock in the nonprofit association that ostensibly was building the houses. Making the down payment a stock purchase avoided wartime credit restrictions.

Buyers got an FHA-guaranteed loan at 4 percent interest. They belonged to the nonprofit building association only while the houses were being built.

The association paid the developers a management fee. Boyar got $44,500 for managing the development of one tract.

296

When the houses were finished, the nonprofit association immediately dissolved and the new houses went into conventional escrow.

The three developers changed their marketing campaign to reassure anxious home buyers.

Don Rochlen's press releases now said the three men were building a $250 million community of "mutual homes."

297

In 1969, Mark Taper said that the three men had made hardly any profit on the houses at all. He said they made only five cents on every dollar they took in.

Taper said the real profit was in developing the commercial lots that Louis Boyar's original plan thoughtfully located no more than a fifteen-minute walk from any house.

298

Louis Boyar and Ben Weingart invested $15,000 of their own money in 1949 to begin building houses on the farmland they had bought with financing from the Prudential Insurance Company.

Robert Young, a railroad financier, and Clint Murchison, the owner of the Del Mar racetrack, put up $300,000 through a syndicate based in Minneapolis. In return, the mortgage syndicate became the exclusive mortgage lender for the houses.

The federal government put up more than $100 million in construction loans and mortgage guarantees.

The transaction was risk-free for Young and Murchison. Both the construction loans and the mortgages were guaranteed under Section 213.

The syndicate made more than $1 million as its share of the profits in developing the subdivision. It also made 4 percent interest on the money it loaned to the three developers. It made another $450,000 in service charges on managing the money it loaned to buyers.

299

Louis Boyar reminded the Senate subcommittee that he had begun his business in 1939 with just $700 in borrowed money.

The subcommittee's legal counsel then asked him to calculate the total value of Boyar's FHA mortgages since 1946.

Boyar calculated rapidly and set the figure at $105 million.

The subcommittee's legal counsel asked Ben Weingart what would happen if any of the dummy corporations defaulted on his $112 million in FHA mortgages.

Weingart said, "I will make the mortgages good."

The subcommittee counsel asked, "Then you will personally endorse the mortgages?"

Weingart said angrily, "No, I will not."

300

According to their Senate testimony, Louis Boyar and Ben Weingart made more than $2 million from constructing just two tracts of "mutual homes" under their interpretation of Section 213.

They made another $1 million on each 600-acre section of empty land they sold to the nonprofit cooperatives they controlled.

The three developers may have made as much as $12 million by the time they dissolved their corporation.

301

Louis Boyar died in 1976, after he had raised billions of dollars for Israel as a cofounder and chairman of Israel Bonds.

He built a high school for gifted children in Jerusalem and named it for his wife. He built the Truman Center for the Advancement of Peace at Hebrew University.

Ben Weingart died in 1980. The charitable foundation he and his wife set up in 1951 gave my city at least $12 million in cash grants and land.

The foundation's gifts came after Weingart had been declared incompetent by a judge, and after his business associates took control of his charitable foundation.

Some of the foundation's gifts came after Weingart was dead.

Weingart's foundation helped construct a community center, a senior citizens center, a library, and a new YMCA.

Mark Taper died in 1994.

Boyar is remembered at the synagogue in my city because his first contributions were to its building fund.

Weingart is remembered because the city gratefully put his name on the community facilities his foundation financed.

Taper is remembered for his gift of either a fish tank—or the fish—at the county library next to city hall.

The librarians don't know which.

302

Mark Taper's charitable foundation donated $1.5 million toward the construction of one of the theaters in the Los Angeles County Music Center.

Ben Weingart's charitable foundation turned the El Rey Hotel on skid row into a shelter and rehabilitation center for the homeless.

303

In 1936, Miriam Clark, the wife of J. Ross Clark, provided the cost of construction for a church in the suburban development her nephew was building.

The Montana Land Company provided the site on Arbor Road.

She gave the church in memory of her son, Walter Clark, who had died on the *Titanic*.

It was a nondenominational church.

304

Some of the men and women in my neighborhood had lived part of their childhood on the outskirts of cotton towns in tents provided by the federal Farm Security Administration.

Some had lived in tarpaper shacks among the oil fields outside of Bakersfield. The shacks didn't have indoor plumbing.

Some had been the first of their family to graduate from high school.

Okies who grew up in California learned to hide their border state twang.

Sometimes, it would reappear after a few drinks among the couples my parents invited over to watch television or play cards.

Some of the couples gave up their Pentecostal religion for milder forms of faith.

They never lost their appreciation for the climate, however. It expressed itself in the fruit trees in the backyards in my neighborhood.

Plums, apricots, oranges, nectarines, and pomegranates were shared over fences in paper bags saved from the grocery store.

305

When I was growing up, to call another boy an Okie, whether he was one or not, would require him to fight.

It was a word that hung in the air between two angry boys like a cocked fist, like the word "nigger."

306

There was very little that distinguished the border Southerners in my neighborhood from my father, who had grown up in Manhattan, or my mother, who had lived on Long Island and worked in New York.

There was very little that distinguished any of us living here.

We lived in what we were told was a good neighborhood.

Our eleven-hundred-square-foot houses were nearly the same.

We shopped at the same stores. We watched the same television programs.

From September to June, my brother and I wore Catholic grade-school uniforms of dark gray corduroy pants, and light gray short-sleeve shirts.

In summer, we wore white cotton T-shirts, denim pants, and high-top tennis shoes. Every boy in my neighborhood did.

Our parents were anxious to do what was expected of them, even when the expectation was not altogether clear.

307

My parents were grateful that they lived among strangers who made about as much money as they did, and who could be counted on, out of friendliness, to help rig a television antenna or dig the footing for a concrete patio.

308

At first, there was no Catholic church in the suburb Louis Boyar, Ben Weingart, and Mark Taper were building, despite what the sales brochure implied.

Mass was said in a movie theater across the street from the Douglas plant.

There was no synagogue either.

In 1952, Boyar had part of the building that housed the subdivision's sales office moved to an empty lot the Jewish community had recently bought. Boyar donated the rest of the building for use as a post office substation.

The temporary building wasn't big enough for a Sunday school. There were too many children.

Rabbi Herbert Rosner set up a network of home schools, staffed by Jewish parents.

The parents assembled in a weekly class to develop a lesson plan for the following Sunday and to learn how to handle a room full of restless children for an hour and a half.

Rabbi Rosner recruited thirty-five parents and enrolled one hundred students. There was a waiting list to enroll more.

309

My father taught in the religious classes offered at our parish church.

The classes were for students who attended public school because their parents couldn't afford the tuition at a Catholic grade school.

On Monday nights, my father taught a class for teenage Catholics who attended public high school.

On Sunday mornings, he went to the county juvenile hall in Downey to instruct young men for their first Communion, something that usually occurs in the second grade.

My father also arranged the more elaborate ceremonies of the year at our parish church. No one else in the parish knew how.

Our parish priests, some ordained in Ireland only a year or two before, were mainly responsible for building a church and the school.

My father had been a member of a religious order. He had been a sacristan and knew the rubrics of the Holy Week services that took place only once a year.

My father instructed the boys who served on the altar, including my brother and me. He explained to the pastor and his assistants how they should walk in procession and what each should do during the ceremony.

On the afternoon before Easter Sunday, he laid out the priests' vestments, the beeswax candles, and the charcoal for lighting the new fire of Easter.

310

My father didn't give very much to the city in which he lived. He didn't join the Lions Club or the Kiwanis.

He didn't coach one of the park sports leagues that the city set up in 1957 to meet the overwhelming demand for recreational activities for children.

He wasn't active in politics.

All twelve thousand names on the petition to incorporate the city in 1954 had to be published in the local newspaper. It took nearly a week to set the type, and cost the backers of incorporation $9,000.

My mother's name was printed in the newspaper. My father hadn't signed the petition.

But after my father's funeral, several people came up to my brother and me and told us that my father had given them advice, or helped them when their marriage was in trouble.

311

Far from anyone he thought might care, my uncle Jack had his body donated to a medical school when he died.

312

My city sponsors an annual awards program for property owners. About four hundred houses are entered in the contest each year.

Teams of volunteers judge the houses on their landscaping, maintenance, and overall appearance.

A volunteer committee, chaired by a city council member, selects grand prize and first place winners.

One of the awards is for a "classic" house—a house hardly changed from one of the models the three developers put up in 1950.

Choosing the houses is difficult.

Selection of a winner comes down to details. Rust stains on the driveway, for instance, may prevent a house from winning a prize.

313

The ceremonies for Holy Thursday include washing the feet of twelve men of the parish in commemoration of Jesus, who had washed the feet of the twelve apostles.

My father arranged for the men to be in the sacristy and directed them to two rows of folding chairs on either side of the altar.

When I was a boy, I served with my brother on Holy Thursday. One of us carried the pitcher that held warm water. The other carried the basin that caught the water poured over each man's right foot.

The foot washing was awkward for both the men and the priest. It required the men to strip off a shoe and sock from a foot that had already been carefully washed at home.

The priest had to bend down, nearly on his hands and knees, to reach the white feet projecting from dark pant legs.

One altar boy positioned the basin under the man's extended foot. The priest poured a small amount of water from the pitcher the other altar boy handed him.

The priest quickly wiped off the water with a towel, stood

up, stepped to the next man, and got down on his knees again.

When my father died, I did not take his place as unofficial sacristan.

I did have my right foot washed on Holy Thursday night.

314

On Good Friday the services are shortened. No mass is said.

The priest and the congregation read one of the gospel accounts of the crucifixion. A narrator reads the descriptions, the priest reads the words of Jesus, and other readers take the parts of Peter and Pontius Pilate.

The congregation reads aloud what the crowds are supposed to have said.

Near the end of the service, after the readings, the congregation participates in the veneration of the cross.

Altar servers bring three or four large crucifixes from the sacristy and take them down to the first step in front of the altar.

Each server holds a crucifix forward, so that the feet of the figure of Jesus on the cross are in reach of someone kneeling on the first step.

Another server holds a small, starched square of white linen.

315

When I was a boy and served on Good Friday, the lines of congregants stretched to the back of the church.

There was no distinction about who could participate in

the veneration of the cross. Mothers and fathers stood with their small children, waiting in line.

They came forward, genuflected briefly on the first step in front of the altar, leaned forward, and kissed the feet of the figure of Jesus on the cross.

If I was holding the cross, I tried to keep it as steady as possible.

If I was holding the square of starched, white cloth, I was supposed to wipe the feet of the figure.

I wasn't sure if this was reverence or something to do with hygiene.

As the members of the congregation venerated the cross, the cloth I carried grew bright red from the lipstick I wiped from the feet of Jesus.

316

While the congregation knelt and venerated the cross, the choir sang.

The hymn the choir sang was *Pange Lingua*, a hymn traditional for Good Friday.

Among its many verses are some addressed to the cross itself.

Dulce lignum,
Dulces clavos,
Dulce pondus sustinet.

Sweet the wood,
Sweet the nails,
Sweet the weight you bear.

PHOTOGRAPHS